A
FEISTY
LITTLE
POINTING
DOG

A
FEISTY
LITTLE
POINTING
DOG

A Celebration of
the Brittany

Edited by David A. Webb

Countrysport Press
Camden / Maine

Line drawings by Christopher Smith

ISBN 0-89272-620-2

Printed at Versa Press, Inc.; Peoria, IL

5   4   3   2   1

Countrysport Press
Camden, ME
www.countrysportpress.com
A Division of Down East Enterprise,
publishers of *Shooting Sportsman* magazine.
www.shootingsportsman.com

Library of Congress Control Number: 2003103168

To my wife Emma and our three sons—
Geoffrey, Daniel, and Joseph—
all of whom have Brittanys. They have tolerated
and, to varying degrees,
enjoyed and participated in my life with the Brittany.
They are my companions and my best friends.

Acknowledgments

The Brittany, a working pointing dog, is the inspiration for each story collected in this volume. The many attributes of the breed are, in fact, the reason that this anthology was assembled. The Brittany has my heartfelt thanks for being the field-trial competitor and hunting companion and true friend that it is.

I owe a debt of gratitude to a number of individuals for their assistance with this project. First and foremost would be Chris Cornell of Down East Books. It was his idea.

I had sent him a query and outline for a different type of book. Along with the submission was a letter with a brief biography indicating my experience with Brittanys. Chris didn't think my original proposal was workable but suggested that I develop an anthology with its central theme being the Brittany.

Next I would like to thank Michael McIntosh for agreeing to write the introduction to A *Feisty Little Pointing Dog*. He has owned several Brittanys and has enjoyed their company both in the field and at home. In addition, Michael gave us permission to use two nicely written stories about his Brittanys.

This volume has been significantly enhanced by Ross Young's cover art and Chris Smith's line drawings. I am very grateful for their creative skills.

Thanks are due, as well, to the authors of the twenty-six stories that are included within the covers of this book. There were fourteen different writers, and with the exception of Ralph Hammond, whom we could not locate, I communicated directly with all of them either by telephone or letter. Universally, they love the Brittany, and all either own, have owned, or have hunted with the breed. Many have more than one Brittany. In fact, Ben O. Williams owns twelve and hunts all of them.

The cooperation and contributions of these fourteen people have been most appreciated.

Finally, I want to thank those individuals who have shared with me so freely their expertise with and knowledge of the Brittany.

Many are past or present members of the Pennsylvania Brittany Club. More than thirty years ago Walt Thompson helped me with our first litter of pups and then showed me how to properly groom a Brittany. Several years later, Dick and Esther Keenan frequently shared their lifelong experiences and wisdom. Esther passed away several years ago. She has been missed by family and friends, but she left with many of us an endearing love for the Brittany. The Keenans' dog Beaupere was one of the first in the United States to attain the titles of dual champion and amateur field champion.

Of equal importance is the information and assistance that Gene Stewart and Jim Waldie have provided me in the field training of the Brittany. Without their help and knowledge, the road to finishing a bird dog and steadying it to wing and shot would have been much rougher.

Others who have given generously of their knowledge include Al and Cindy Cropek, Kevin O'Brien, Chris Rider, Tom Tracy, Gregg Sackett, and George Sweeney. Thank you all.

—David Webb

List of Authors

David Brooks
Martha H. Greenlee
C. W. Gusewelle
David Guterson
Ralph Hammond
Tom Hennessey
David Kenney
Lois J. Mannon
Bill McClure
Michael McIntosh
Steven Mulak
Steve Savage
Tred Slough
Charley Waterman
David Webb
Ben O. Williams

Contents

Foreword

Great dog stories can tug at your heartstrings and cause you to reflect on your very soul. They can make you laugh and remember special moments in time. Collected within these covers are twenty-six stories that focus on one breed of pointing dog—the Brittany.

Detailed descriptions of the Brittany are available in various reference works, but these often list only the physical attributes of the breed. The real character of the Brittany is in the pages that follow. It's in the stories of the men and women who train, hunt, and compete in the field with their Brittanys.

Each author has his or her own unique perspective on the Brittany. In his introduction, Michael McIntosh describes the Brit as a poachers' dog, then tells us that his Ginny, Katie, and October were all actually poachers because they stole his heart.

Novelist David Guterson writes about a chukar hunt in the Columbia River Basin of central Washington state. Excerpted from his book *East of the Mountains*, this tale portrays the novel's lead character in pursuit of the mountain bird with his two Brittanys. From the extraordinarily descriptive writing, you just know that David Guterson "has been there and done that."

Several of the authors have done more than just hunting with their Brittanys. Martha Greenlee and Lois Mannon are active horseback field trialers. Steve Mulak has both competed in and judged field trials. Although Bill McClure hunts more than sixty days a season in his beloved Ontario grouse and woodcock coverts, he has also been active in field trials and has shown his Brittanys. Several of his dogs have achieved the ultimate goal of being dual bench and field champions.

Dave Books has hunted extensively throughout the Midwest and Northwest; Steve Savage has concentrated his efforts in the state of Utah; Dave Kenney prefers to chase quail in Illinois and neighboring states; while Robert Holthouser (d.b.a.Tred Slough) most often pursues grouse in the southern Blue Ridge Mountains of the Carolinas.

Charles Gusewelle and Tom Hennessey have each contributed a story that pays tribute to a late Brittany whose personality and field performance are sorely missed. And that is exactly what this anthology is all about—a celebration of and tribute to the Brittany.

Over the years, Charley Waterman and Ben O. Williams have had a unique relationship. Charley has begged and borrowed several of Ben's Britts to work before his gun. These occasions are portrayed in three of the stories written by these two gifted authors.

Finally, if you have ever looked into the eyes of a dog (in this case a Brittany), closely observed various canine traits, and seen smudges on window glass from the dogs who travel in your car, you will undoubtedly relate to the three brief pieces that I, myself, have written.

Enjoy.

—David Webb

Introduction

by Michael McIntosh

They were poachers' dogs, or so legend has it: compact and biddable, close-working and quiet, the perfect accomplice for clandestine sport and the companion of choice among those whose favorite game was someone else's.

I don't know whether the legend is true, but I do know that Brittanys themselves are shameless poachers. They'll steal your favorite chair, your wife's affections, your lunch, and your heart.

Although I've been around pointing dogs since I was born and have hunted upland birds over them since I was old enough to carry a gun, I did not meet a Brittany till I was twenty-four. My father hunted with pointers. Most of his partners hunted with pointers, and those who didn't had setters. I knew one man who had a Viszla and another who had a Weimaraner, but if there was anyone in southeastern Iowa who hunted with a Brittany, I never ran into him.

In the summer of 1970, I completed a graduate degree and landed a teaching job at a small state college in St. Joseph, Missouri. For digs, I rented one side of a duplex at the very edge of town. Out back were old, hilly pastures, and across the road, John Zook lived on what these days would be called a hobby farm. Except that John's real hobby had less to do with a few acres of corn than with the rambling kennel and big exercise yard that stood east of the house.

But what breed were these? Gun dogs obviously, just

from the way they moved, but beyond that I was mystified. They were small, stub tailed, orange and white, handsome. And decidedly amiable, as I learned when I walked up to the fence, leaving the U-Haul truck idling in my driveway. I was met by a row of sweet faces jockeying for pets and the rubbing of ears.

Next day, I noticed a man puttering around the kennel, so I went over, introduced myself, and asked what kind of dogs these were.

"Brit'nys," John said in his clipped way of speaking. "Quail dogs."

Ah. I still wasn't sure what a "Brit'ny" was, but quail dogs I understood—though I suspect that in those first moments John figured anybody who didn't recognize a Brit'ny wouldn't know a quail from a quadrille.

"You hunt quail?" I asked. He admitted he did.

"Me, too," I said.

He gave me a skeptical look. "Yeah? Whaddya shoot?"

"L.C. Smith twenty."

The skeptical look faded a bit. "Where ya from?"

"Southern Iowa."

The look disappeared, replaced by a smile.

And so in one stroke I found the first hunting partner in my newly adopted state and the dogs that would own my heart. Now, thirty years later, I live in another newly adopted state, and I've enjoyed the company of many other hunting partners since. But my heart still belongs to Brittanys.

Gradually, as we hunted together over John's main man, Sport, and as I hung around his kennel, I began to learn a few things about these dogs that somehow captivated me as no other breed ever had: They are the only breed of spaniels that point (in those days, they were still called Brittany Spaniels); they were developed in France and first brought to the United States in the 1920s; they are natural retrievers; some are born tailless; and their genetic wiring is by no means set in stone. John had one litter of five, all males, that at two months were perfect stairsteps— no two of the same height or weight. If you look in the chapter titled "Not Yesterday I Learned to Know the Love," you'll read about Katie, who didn't look like any Brittany you probably ever saw and was certainly not like any I've ever seen, before or since.

You'll find there, too, that my first Brittany did not come from John Zook's kennel but rather from Illinois, on a phone call and a whim. At least it seemed like a whim at the time. Now, however, I have to wonder if it wasn't something more on the order of predestination, because every gun dog that has lived at my house in the years since has been a Brittany.

And I've met a lot of others along the way. A few haven't struck me as overly bright, and a few others weren't much account as hunters, but I have never met a Brittany who was mean-spirited or standoffish. It's as if the best qualities of canine nature are so thoroughly fundamental to the breed that they just can't help but show it. To someone who loves all dogs, a Brittany in a way *is* all dogs.

Which is not to say they aren't at times perverse or willful or capable of behavior that makes you get red in the face and use coarse language. But that, too, is canine nature, and though you don't have to love it, you'll at least accept it.

I don't believe Brittanys are for every hunter. Their nature is to work relatively close to the gun and a bit more slowly than some other breeds. While that suits my temperament and perhaps yours, it's not everyone's cup of tea. That's why there's more than one breed of gun dog—and why I disagree so deeply with certain breeders and trainers who over the past twenty-odd years have sought to make Brittanys into field-trial dogs that can compete against the hard-running breeds that hunt from horizon to horizon. As I see it, if you want the performance of an English pointer, buy an English pointer. A Brittany is fire and silk; if the fire doesn't burn quite as hot as in some other breeds, and if the silk is rather softer, what of it? That's their charm. That's why I love them so.

And it's why I take a quietly fiendish pleasure in the way things work out sometimes.

~ ~

When she was twelve, the one I named October became a half-day dog, though she didn't know it. Her face was gray, her eyes were going cloudy, and the old spark was fading to embers. Her last all-day hunt was for quail on a north-Missouri farm that belongs to an old friend. It was a good year for birds, the habitat was superb, and my partner's brace of strong young setters coursed it beautifully. But it was one of those days when the quail were someplace other than where they should have been, and I drove home that night with the sweet recollection that the only two coveys we got to shoot at over honest points belonged to a crotchety, puttery old lady who'd complained incessantly the night before because she'd had to sleep in the kennel with the other dogs rather than her usual place, in bed next to me.

It was her way, all of it—the putzy style, the fundamental belief that she was entitled to be wherever the hell she wanted to be, and the ready willingness to bitch about any slight, real or perceived, at the top of her lungs. I did at least as much to create that attitude as I later did to curb it, so in the spirit of fair play, she allowed me to be in charge often enough that I was able to retain some measure of dignity in the relationship, even though she taught me that there's no use pretending to be any better than I am. Since she left, I have never felt more keenly the truth of Burton Spiller's lament that the life of a dog is not as long as the life of a man.

Tober grew truly old, unable to hunt. But the desire never really goes away, so during her last two seasons she went along as always, tottered around for a half-hour sniffing everything, then was happy to go back into her crate for a snooze while I went hunting.

The dogs tell you when it's time, when they're no longer happy to be here.

I will not soon forget the eighth of September 1998—neither the events nor the measure of symmetry involved. Twenty-eight years after herding a U-Haul truck into Missouri and walking across a gravel road to meet some captivating dogs, I drove another U-Haul into a new driveway in South Dakota. Tober had ridden for two days with me, sprawled on the seat with her head in my lap, as content to be there as she was chagrined at having to be lifted in and out.

She was perkier than usual the day we unloaded, pottering around underfoot or lying close by in benign supervision. That night, I carried her up the stairs, and she settled onto a buffalo robe I folded next to the bed. Next morning, as if something vital had fled silently, inexplicably into the darkness, she couldn't even lift her head.

In a new and unfamiliar place, a thousand miles from what had so recently been home, Vicky went out to find a vet while I sat on the floor next to the old girl, absorbing what I knew was an inescapable truth. I stroked her, knowing that as long as she could feel my hands she would not feel the fear that was knotting in my gut like a slowly gathering ball of ice.

I talked to her, told her once again what a beautiful puppy she'd been and how grateful I was for the more than fifteen years we were together. And I told her some things that only she was meant to hear.

An hour later, she was gone, lying on a stainless-steel table, still cradled in my arms when Dr. Larry Stoddard found the vein.

The rest is partly blurred but partly still so vivid that it crimps my throat—the drive to a Rapid City veterinary clinic that offers cremation, the ineffable sadness of touching her—now rigid and cold—one last time, of murmuring a last good-bye before turning away to face the rest of my life and the knowledge that it would never again be quite the same.

Poacher's dogs.

They'll steal your heart.

A
FEISTY
LITTLE
POINTING
DOG

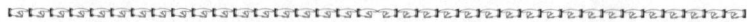

DAVID GUTERSON grew up in Seattle, Washington, and has spent all his life in the Northwest. He currently lives with his wife and family on an island in Puget Sound. After receiving his B.A. and M.A. degrees from the University of Washington, he taught high-school English for many years.

He is a contributing editor to *Harper's* magazine, and his stories and articles have appeared in other publications such as *Sports Illustrated,* the *Los Angeles Times* magazine, and *Newsweek.* He has written several books including *The Country Ahead of Us, The Country Behind,* which is a collection of short stories, as well as the best-selling novels *Snow Falling on Cedars* and *East of the Mountains.*

When he's not writing, David goes afield in pursuit of upland birds with a Brittany or two.

Chukars in October Light is an edited excerpt from the novel, *East of the Mountains* (first edition released in 1999). Permission to use it in this anthology was given by both the author, David Guterson, and the publisher, Harcourt, Inc.

Chukars in October Light

by David Guterson

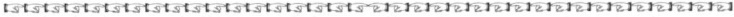

He set free his Brittanys, Rex and Tristan, and they quartered ahead, into the desert country. Ben went after them, traversing uphill, climbing the breaks above the river. Putting discomfort out of his mind, he passed between rough bands of basalt stained in pale streaks with bird droppings. Twice he stopped to ease his breath and rest half-bent with his palms against his knees. Far below lay the bridge he'd crossed and the silver-tinted river. He could see the dam at Wanapum, the sun pale in the southern sky, the canyon walls scalloped and scoured, the petrified drift of the basalt flows. He could see the drifter, still hitchhiking. To the north the river narrowed again and squeezed between bland rock walls before disappearing around a bend. The prairie smelled of sage and of the dampness held in the earth. Overhead the vast expanse of sky ran so deeply and unbroken to blue that he felt a momentary vertigo.

He hunted northward in open country, following the broken line of the ridgetop, the river running below him in the west, the dogs working at a cross angle to the soft October breeze. Rabbit brush and purple sage festooned the bunchgrass prairie. A dozen times the dogs flushed flitting sparrows, who at the last minute bolted forward into far-off patches of cover. Rex would roust them out once more and send them in spurts of three or four, banging like popcorn out of the sage, then away across the hills. The shadow of a hawk passed over the land, and then the hawk bore down in lazy circles, caught the swelling river breezes, and rode broadside across the breaks, working south with ease. Ben stopped, slipped free of his rucksack, and drank from his water bottle. He felt broken in, less raw and fragile, though a ligament behind his left knee seemed bound up from the steepness of the climb, and in his left hip joint there was bone-against-bone clicking and sliding beneath the fascia. Yet vaguely he felt improved by the high air. The desert fragrance had cleaned his sinuses. He rested, fingered his side, and soon rose to hunt again over the breaks behind his pointing dogs.

It was early evening, the light fallen low, when he came across his first chukars. The air had cooled with the dying of the sun, and the birds were on the move to forage on the succulent blades and seeds of bunchgrass growing along the ridge crest. As they fed, they separated and called to one another reassuringly; Ben heard their gregarious, staccato clucking before his dogs could catch their scent riding on the wind. He stopped to listen and to fix their location. He cradled the shotgun in the crook of his arm and called the dogs in close. He listened with his palm cupped around his ear, turning his head down the long route of the horizon. The chukars, he thought, were feeding to the north, though with them there was no real certainty, for their low fast call always seemed to Ben to come from everywhere at once.

He had not pushed ahead more than thirty paces when Tristan became hotly agitated. The dog raised his snout to the breeze and trotted forward twenty yards, and with this the chukars stopped calling. Rex cut hard and fast behind Tristan, down into the breaks to follow scent where no doubt the birds had laid up through the heat before abandoning their cover for the ridge crest. It was silent now. Ben moved up between the dogs and dug in his thumb against the safety tang. Tristan had gone all stalkingly tight and was edging right and left again. Ben understood that when the birds broke at last, they would hurl themselves cleverly over the break and he would have the low sun in his eyes. He held his shotgun lightly. Rex bounded up into view from below with his withers flattened and his ears back. The dogs worked aprowl before him with their noses trailing fresh ground scent, and Ben stopped to collect himself, should the birds suddenly flush. He relocated forward, set his feet, and adjusted the tilt of his sunglasses. He had just swung his rucksack onto the ground when Tristan halted twenty yards out and locked up high at both ends beautifully, classically gone on point.

Ben edged tensely forward. "Stay where you are," he said to Rex, who had not stopped pounding insatiably through the cover as if to put up all the birds. The dog, against his will, held up.

Then everything was still and silent. Ben had time to think. In his teenage years it had been his habit to pass on the initial shot at chukars, since they always posted a sentry, like the guard cow in a band of feeding elk. The first bird often flushed wild at a distance from where the feeding covey would then flush outside of shooting range. More than that practicality, there was something poignant in passing on a first shot and standing in silence while the bird fled. There was something haunting in it.

When the lone bird got up at last, it held low to the

purple sage, and in the late October light Ben saw plainly its dark barred markings, its vermilion feet, and its chestnut tail feathers. There was the quiet stirring of a single bird's wings while swiftly the chukar dropped over the breaks and sailed out freely above the river, where suddenly it grew incidental and disappeared down the hill.

Immediately the dogs moved forward, as though the flushed bird had been a shadow. Ben worked wide to his right and ahead so that the shots he might take would be more direct and less like passing shots. In the next moment, the two Brittanys went on point together, a few yards apart in a patch of high bunchgrass, Rex pitched leftward with one paw raised, Tristan low and stretched solidly. Ben flicked off his safety and calmed his reeling heart.

It was always at this moment that he hesitated to take the life of a bird. It had been this way since he was eight years old, shooting mourning doves alongside his father. It had been easier for him in his teenage years.

Ben stood waiting for the birds to flush. A chukar got up under Rex's nose, winging low toward the river breaks, and he shot it with the open barrel bored as if for shooting skeet. Suddenly chukars were everywhere, leaving cover in a bold flush, a dozen or more leaping from the bunch-grass while Ben was frozen by the weight of his astonishment and swung through on one bird and then another. At last he gave out with the second barrel, which was choked down tightly for a distant shot, and the chukar rose higher on the wing, as if assailed by a fast-rising breeze, and sailed wounded toward the sagebrush.

Down the breaks below his feet, the remaining chukars settled. Ben knew they would sit for a lonesome interlude and finally in frantic desperation call with a yearning to meet again, until the covey reassembled. He wanted to hunt them while they were likely to hold, waiting for him to pass by.

He worked Tristan after the cripple. When the dog maneuvered close enough, the wounded chukar abandoned cover and dragged its left wing through the sage. Ben felt sullied by what had happened and watched helplessly while Tristan gave chase, pounced to seize the running bird, and clutched it softly between his teeth in a puff of gently floating feathers.

At the crest of the breaks Ben stood, bird in hand, and watched while Rex brought the other slain chukar in and laid it neatly on the table rock. He praised his dogs, though not too profusely, as they stood panting at his side. Ben slid the first bird into his coat pocket and picked up the second to examine it, a young male with small, rounded spurs. He tucked it in beside the first.

The sun lay low against the mountains, but there was still good shooting light. He slid off his sunglasses, fingered the dressing over his eye, and worked on his steel-rimmed glasses. He drank some water—he emptied one bottle—and then he went after the singles slowly, leaving his rucksack behind on the ground, urging the dogs to stay close.

Last hunt, he told himself.

He hunted three hundred feet downhill. He missed on the first flush, but then there were others, and he felt satisfied. One bird he took straightaway on a second shot, staying beneath it as it barreled downhill; the next flushed from behind a stone tower and, unlike most chukars he'd seen as a boy, flew toward him along a steady contour twenty yards below his gun, so that he had to swing patiently for the longest time and kill it on the late going away.

He held this last bird in his hand. A dark band passed rakishly over its eyes, and the black bars along its flanks lay symmetrically, sleekly ruffled. The tail feathers were chestnut brown and the feathers elsewhere an olive color, in places darker or a blue-tinted gray; they lay well-ordered in delicate waves and were soft and thick against its breast. The warmth of life was still in it.

Ben put the bird in his coat pocket. He climbed the breaks in the last light of day with a steady pain in his side. The day was closing around him now. Things could not hold light any longer. Weary of climbing, short of breath, he paid no attention to his hunting dogs. The darkness seeped into and over the land, and inevitably into Ben too, as he saw the world swallowed by night.

He was too tired and in too much pain for the long hike back into Vantage. He sat and waited for things to improve, but there was only the sweep of the night wind blowing and the discord of his breathing. Reluctantly, he climbed fifty feet, and fifty more, until he came to his rucksack.

Now Ben breasted one of the chukars and fed the boned meat to his dogs. He tossed the remains of the bird down the hill; he watered his dogs from his aluminum cup, pouring a ration for each. He spread the duffel bag and the rain poncho on the ground, stuffed the remaining chukars in his rucksack, and lay down wrapped up tightly in his blanket like a nomad in the desert.

Ben's dogs excavated and maneuvered in the sand, settling in at his side. He urged them closer for the warmth they could provide. It was good to have them near, companions. They were sentinels, too, beside him there in the frigid, inhospitable night.

BILL McCLURE and his wife, Kathryn, live in ruffed grouse country near Manotick, Ontario. Bill has bred, trained, competed with, and hunted Brittanys for forty years. His current three females are line descendants of the first dog he and Kathryn owned.

A successful field trialer and judge in both the United States and Canada, Bill has been a lifelong bird hunter. He and his dogs spend more than sixty days each season in their favorite grouse and woodcock coverts.

An outdoor writer and photographer by profession, Bill is a columnist for *Gun Dog, Wildfowl,* and *The American Hunter* magazines and has contributed to many other publications.

The stories *Anniversaries, Milestones,* and *Gone But Not Forgotten* were originally published in *Gun Dog* in August/September 1995, August/September 1996, and June/July 1996, respectively. Permission to use the stories in this anthology was given by the author, Bill McClure.

Anniversaries

by Bill McClure

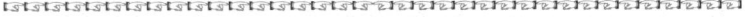

She was born thirty-five years ago, and her life influenced me enormously. Without her, I doubt that I would have become so deeply committed to dogs and shooting, even though long before her birth I was an incurable gunner. But watching her grow and helping her learn, while learning myself, was a watershed experience in my life. Champion and Field Champion Kipewa's Breton Belle and I were together for fifteen years. A Brittany, she was a very good gun dog. We were devoted to one another. Her spirit and the lessons I learned while in her company have been part of me ever since. Sadly, no dog has ever reached thirty-five years of age, but Kip lives in my memories.

In the old coverts I hunt there are times when I think of her. A few years ago I was sure I heard her special handmade Nova Scotia brass bell, even though I could also hear clearly the beeper worn by her great-granddaughter, with whom I was hunting. The sound of that familiar tinkling ran right up by the rail fence toward the young poplars, as if it was thirty years ago. I almost expected to find Kip on point.

In another premier grouse cover, which has changed little in twenty-five years thanks to its sandy soil and periodic cattle grazing, I can still see her standing a grouse from a position on an alder knoll, her breath condensing in the October air. That was the covert where one time she pointed a second grouse while retrieving the first. One day in this glen, in the company of a friend and his daughter, Kip pointed over thirty grouse in three hours. There were no mistakes. That was one of her favorite places—and mine too. She flew from knoll to knoll, from clump to clump, and from grouse to grouse. A master at work.

Although adept on ruffed grouse, Kip enjoyed the woodcock flights. Naturally cautious when she detected scent, my Brittany would nevertheless proceed rapidly into the cone and cease movement just at the correct instant. That makes for clean work and confidence. Kip virtually taught herself steadiness to wing and shot. Though, like us, she had her moments when enthusiasm resulted in a loss of manners, Kip's intentions were always good. If she broke when a bird got up, it was out of unendurable frustration and pent-up emotion—not willful disobedience. Then she felt disgraced and sought forgiveness.

Once, when shooting woodcock with a friend, we lost Kip on point. Although her bell had stopped close by in a thicket, our exhaustive search failed to turn up my dog. I called, blew the whistle, and marched up and down the brush, focusing my mind and eyes on what an orange-and-white dog would look like in the brown-and-yellow brush. Finally, my companion and I came together in despair. That moment was similar to the one following the burst of a November white-tailed deer from cover, when the suddenness of its vanishing makes you wonder if it was ever really there. You question your senses. I called several more times in a plaintive tone.

Then we heard it. A gentle tinkle at first, as if her neck was barely moving the bell, and then the sound of the bell heading toward me. In a moment she was in sight of us. When Kip saw me and I acknowledged her, she wheeled around and went back, pointing where she had been. We flushed her bird and killed it as it topped the brush. Events like that never leave your memory.

A year later in the same covert, a few hundred yards from the lost-on-point woodcock incident, in a more mature softwood stand, Kip locked up. When my friend and I arrived at her side, a grouse jumped close from under a fallen log and we shot it. Kip remained staunch and refused to move. I stepped forward to touch her and encourage her to release when two woodcock flushed five feet to her left. We bagged them, but Kip remained still. A second later, another grouse rose from under the leaning pine, greeted with the bang of a shotgun. Its fall broke the tension, and Kip retrieved it.

Kip's introduction to game birds at six months of age in 1960 was confined to Hungarian partridge. They were abundant in our oat and pasture fields, and in the meadows across from our house. Kip taught herself—and me—how and where to locate and handle coveys in the open farmland of eastern Ontario. At two years of age she was winning field trials on wild Huns. Her range, although never carrying her out of touch with me, took her great distances in search of birds. As her experience grew, she covered all four field corners while the gunners walked the middle. When we were a few rods into a stubble, Kip moved on to the next objective. She saw hundreds of coveys during her early years in the training areas near the city, which then held five to twelve groups in several hundred acres. In August or September, our Sunday or evening workouts were always alive with action.

Kip was a lucky dog, and I was a lucky master—in more ways than one. Even though I had owned several dogs previously, in retrospect I was terribly inexperienced. She and I got to know one another intimately from our constant contact and mutual observation. I learned by trial and error how to deal with situations I had never seen before. Praise be that I owned a forgiving dog who, in spite of all her bird-finding desire, wanted to please and never required force or coercion but instead responded to a change in tone of voice like some dogs might to the whip.

I erred often in her development and once nearly ruined her. Kip was not much more than two years old when I hunted her in an area that usually held a half-dozen Hun coveys. Sure enough, in the third field, she established a stand. When I approached, a covey rose out of range. For some inexplicable reason, Kip broke. En route to the distant covey, which lit a half-mile away, my gun dog alternately pointed and flushed two more coveys and eventually got up the first one.

After running Kip down, I scolded and punished her. When I turned to pick up my gun, she hightailed it back to the truck a mile away. When I arrived at the vehicle, Kip was hiding under it. That lesson has never left me. When I pass the area—now a huge subdivision with two malls—I remember that incident. Kip did not hold a grudge, but my conduct was inappropriate.

Later that autumn, I watched her close in on a moving covey in a short pasture, stop, correct, and move forward swiftly, only to jam up again. This was repeated three times. Kip carried her head high, probing the airborne scent. Her's was not a pushing-pottering-nudging of a covey. These were clean relocations on a running flock that decided they weren't going to hold. My heart was in my throat when, once more, Kip pointed, but a moment later she abandoned her stand to execute a wide swing out into the field and then an arc back in front and toward me. A hundred yards out, she stopped. I walked forward and flushed the covey jammed between us. I haven't seen that since.

One of the nicest comments about Kip came from Richard Johns, a famous field trial judge, professional trainer, and gentleman, who said, "She spends her whole time away out there looking for a bird to point—for you." Nicky Bissell, a legendary figure in Brittany circles, rode up to us after my little grouse dog conducted herself with skill and dignity in the Brittany National Championships, held in quail fields near Carbondale, Illinois. She said, "I wish I owned her."

I am honored that I did. In her first dog show, the judge, a famous New Yorker, suggested that I trot her on the inside so he could look at the dog rather than me! I corrected my handling error and Kip, the only Brittany in the Sporting Group, placed second. She won her field championship in an all-breed trial on released pheasants, but she failed to find a ringneck. Instead, after a dozen dogs had passed an alder thicket halfway around the course, she located a single woodcock there and handled it perfectly. Both of us were very proud. So were the judges, whose task she made easy. The next day, in the same trial and in another released-bird event, she found two grouse! Her daughter won the derby stake. That was the weekend of October 16, 1965—thirty-year-old memories.

Later that month, my new champion and I visited Grouse Alley and then went over to the Stone Bridge cover, where she handled five woodcock and nine grouse. Kip easily adapted from a field trial to a gunning trip. On the morning of October 25, 1966, she found four birds in the covert behind our house. Three days later, Kip won the Brittany Grouse Classic at Ipswich, Massachusetts, in a field of twenty-two. Here is what was written about that: "Kipewa's Breton Belle turned in a sterling performance— fleet of foot and light in step as she coursed her country with high-headed purpose. At twenty-seven minutes she

proved her manners as she probed a pine stand and voluntarily backed her bracemate. At forty minutes she failed to show along the swamp bottom. She was found statuesquely indicating the presence of a grouse. All was in good order as it winged away and the shot rang out."

We were back to the grouse coverts and the Hun fields of eastern Ontario in a few days, which is exactly where both of us belonged. And that's where we stayed until she could no longer make her body do what her mind wanted. Along the way there were more field trial victories and many triumphs with game birds. Then her children and their children took over. To this day, my hunting dogs have her name multiple times in their pedigrees.

Nineteen ninety-five is quite the anniversary year. Thirty-five years ago I began seriously learning about gun dogs as one of Kip's pupils. Five years before that, I married a postgraduate student and a Nova Scotia coal miner's daughter, Kathryn Skinner, who for two score years has shared the joys and tears of gun-dog/human relationships. It was Kathryn who chose Kip from the litter a friend and I had bred. It was Kathryn who cared for the dogs, fed them, nursed them in sickness, and comforted them in whelp. In my absence she held the elderly and sick while our vet put them to sleep, and she has been by my side when we laid them to rest. All that and four children, community-leadership responsibilities, and her own work. We got our first gun dog within weeks of our wedding and have never been without several since. Our four children now own dogs.

When I was away on business it was Kathryn who took the dogs for runs, and on one notable occasion Sal and King engaged a flock of the neighbor's ducks, which were waddling to the brook. King, Kip's son, himself a champion, retrieved one to hand. The price of the deceased was negotiated. Another time two litters of pups that Kathryn was exercising on the lawn spied our children's flock of Bantam hens, Henny Penny and Chicken Little, accompanied by their groom, Roderick, and two clutches of chicks. The ensuing chase, which involved twenty-two chicks, two cackling hens, one crowing rooster, plus fourteen puppies, and four children, is recounted to this day at family gatherings. Through it all, Kathryn laughed and coped.

My gun dogs accompanied her shopping, sitting up in the front seat like cats in a coal box. On more than one occasion, when the furry passengers were left guarding the groceries, crimes took place. Once, on a Christmas Eve day trip to the village, the sainted Kip remained in the car to watch over several wrapped packages of special Christmas cookies. When Kathryn returned, the cookies were no more, and our champion had crumbs on her face.

It is said that every woman during her lifetime is entitled to one good dog and one good man. Kathryn believes we have had many good dogs. She doesn't remember a bad one. That's her nature. Any comment on the "one good man" I will leave to her, but I must say that although I have never been awarded a show and performance title, neither have I stolen her Christmas cookies. Not in forty years.

Milestones

by Bill McClure

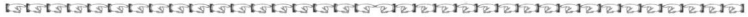

This year is the occasion of *Gun Dog*'s fifteenth anniversary, and we celebrated with another important event. Late on April 30 and on into the early hours of May 1, three ladies and one gentleman repeatedly called our Brittany "Chip" a "sweetie." Chip is many things, but I don't believe any of those she admires have ever thought of her so endearingly; certainly not the grouse, woodcock, Huns, red-winged blackbirds, squirrels, chipmunks, or marmots. They all recognize her as a consummate and patient predator, not a "sweetie."

These touching descriptions took place over a period of many hours while Chip reclined on a pile of clean towels on the basement floor of our veterinarian's clinic. Nature's intention was that she whelp puppies. Medical observation was indicated because the first pup in the chute had a large cranium and for a while stubbornly blocked the passage of his siblings. A little massage from a skilled lady vet, and out he came. His following brother was so greatly relieved to see light at the end of the tunnel that he uttered a tiny cry of joy while still deep inside his mother. Before dawn, five more followed the blocker. These proceedings were monitored by two midwives, one of vast experience, and both possessed of great compassion. Two medical advisors checked Chip and remained on call. Every two hours or so another pup slipped out, into the waiting hands of Chip's handlers. After the second birth our first-time mother caught on to what was required of her and fulfilled her maternal duties with enthusiasm. Each time she pushed, groaned, grunted, or winced, one or more of her assistants referred to her tenderly as "sweetie." Sometimes all present repeated in sequence this term of endearment.

With all these caring, willing, and competent hands on the floor with my dog, I selected a perch on a director's chair a few feet away from the parturition. From this vantage point I had Chip's eye and added appropriate words of encouragement and praise for her devotion to the pups already squeaking at her breasts. An unsolicited but enthusiastic stream of announcements were forthcoming from her caregivers as to each new arrival's sex, cuteness, markings, and vitality. All were, within a minute of birth, pronounced perfect. What with all this excitement and running commentary, I occupied my mind worrying about Chip's health while silently composing a variety of prayers for her deliverance from any problems. By dawn the next morning my invocation was answered. A proud mother, four daughters, and two sons reclined at home in peace and health in the whelping box in which Chip and her mother, Nick, and Nick's mother, Corky, had been born. Each of these maternal ancestors plus four more take us back forty years.

My gun dogs have had many strengths and widely admired personality traits and each was a competent hunter. Some were exceptional in the field and a few were, if a Brittany can ever be so regarded, quite handsome. Several were noted competitors racking up lots of field trial victories. All possessed friendly, happy, generous personalities with people and dogs. None were born tailless in spite of what you may read about this characteristic being common. It is not. The commonality is how the ill-informed repeat the error they read in someone else's article.

All my gun dogs have been delighted to break off a hunt to come back and join me in urination. One author scoffed at this Brittany trait but I consider my dog's attendance at what they see as territorial marking to be a representation of pack solidarity. I have always admired loyalty in dogs and friends including its manifestation during urination. Maybe we should commend this behavior to politicians. It would be more becoming than many of their public activities and much more so than some they believe they are conducting in private.

Chip is a dog my grandson affectionately described as "a nut case." When a five year old who is helping grandpa train the dogs identifies such a trait you can be assured you are onto something. Let me illustrate: A few years ago during a woodcock shoot, my shooting partner had to unload his 28 gauge before rolling in laughter on the October leaves when Chip, during her first season, located a downed woodcock she had pointed and we had shot. Her intensity is the strongest I have ever seen. Heaven and Earth can't move her. Nor could we that October morn. With the bird only inches from her nose there was our gun dog riveted with every neuron sparking with enough electrical energy to start a truck. She seemed willing to starve herself to death in the covert unless either the bird moved or we removed it. When I reached down to pick it up, Chip didn't blink an eye until the scent cone vanished. She was in a trance.

And there is more: Last spring while carrying the puppies, she discovered a window ledge bird feeder I had installed in March. A variety of song birds, three pairs of doves, and several squirrels and chipmunks visited the station. From the kitchen doorway, eleven feet from the window the expectant mother would, until corrected, be found immobile cast like a bronze-and-white statue. Glutton that she is, even meal time was ignored. Twice I found her perched on the telephone chair by the window glass transfixed with her nose separated from a chipmunk by the thickness of the thermopane. Not a muscle moved. I thought she would disintegrate. What a wonderful in utero experience for her babies. Regrettably I have been away from chipmunk shooting since childhood but it appears there could be a future in it.

In utero pointing and predatory lessons were not the only experiences to which the six embryos were exposed. The woodcock came back in early April to be greeted with snow, cold, and generalized misery. The timely arrival of the migrant songbirds was similarly saluted by unspeakable weather. Our eastern Phoebes arrived here looking for bugs and nearly froze to death. The woodcock hatched in a blizzard. Through it all the wildflowers arrived more or less on schedule but their growth was slowed by the sunless cold. Finally in mid-May the temperature got into the sixties.

But back in March, Chip, her unborn, her sister P.D., and I experienced an astonishing wildlife event. On a night when the temperature was below freezing and a light snowfall had whitened the ground I took Chip and her sister out for a last turn around the yard before retiring. It was mild with little or no wind. The wet snow fell gently. Then I heard the introductory roll, followed by the unmistakable sound of a male ruffed grouse in full drumming. It was 10:15 P.M. on a black night in March! It was snowing!

A few days later the drummer appeared from the woods surrounding our house to take a bedtime snack under another bird feeder located in the middle of the yard. He visited nightly and often for breakfast. These visits could be viewed from the chair, but Chip preferred a pointing position with her snout twisted on the glass of the back storm door. My dog might still be there except the vigil was interrupted by labor contractions. It is a miracle the first pup wasn't born on the stoop.

It will be interesting to see how she helps her family learn the basics of proper field comportment and obedience. Chip's mother "The Nick" was a very patient, willing, and attentive instructor. When her family was young she eagerly showed them the rewards that came from obedience, and on other occasions she demonstrated the fleeting pleasures derived from a few moments of disobedience. Nick had many attributes and her mistakes were always performed with such enthusiasm that they were easily overlooked. She was born fifteen years ago just weeks before the first issue of *Gun Dog* was printed and lived a long healthy, active, and vigorous sporting life. In an early issue of *Gun Dog* I described her training during the period when the horizon was the limit and a whistle was considered an owner's musical instrument. One incident I recalled was Nick's appearance at the edge of a standing cornfield following a long absence and much whistle blowing. She spied me but simultaneously located a dead skunk. He won out. Nick was never one to pass up a spine-twisting roll in ripe offal.

Nor was her mother Corky whose specialty in hare

coursing is unsurpassed in our seven generations of Brittanys. Corky wins; by a big margin, too, for not only was she talented, but in spite of every known correction including a couple that wouldn't pass a knee-jerk animal rights committee, she continued the pastime until her deathbed. She was also a very good bird dog, a natural soft retriever, and everyone's friend. Jack Clark an Ontario Brittany professional who knew Corky as a gun dog once said he wished he owned her. I was glad I did. An interesting offshoot of her hare tracking talent was very thorough work on a wounded running bird. They never escaped.

Back in 1980 I shot a grouse that glided down into a patch of dense cover obscured by conifers. After a long search with my setter, we came up empty. Although the cover was miles from home, I went back three days later with Corky. We had no luck. Two days more elapsed and I took her there again. Within forty yards she hit scent, pointed, broke, and took a trail. Deep in the slash there was a scuffle and in came Corky bearing the winged grouse. But with all her ability and a winning personality, Corky had her off days. One of these is recorded in my diary dated November 17, 1980. At a productive and important covert, my dear Corky ran up four grouse from under the hawthorn bushes, then chased two from the base of an apple tree, and finally didn't even notice a whitetail doe, which nearly ran over her. My displeasure was recorded: "She was oblivious to everything. No birds—thanks to a stupid little dog." But a year later, when *Gun Dog* was new, Corky handled nine birds perfectly, three in a hedge and six in the raspberry canes and my remarks claim: "We were pleased to come home with three."

On November 16, 1981, Corky, according to my notes,

"had a perfect location and point on a grouse which I missed in the open with both barrels. Shame. She found a second. I repeated my performance. This was followed by two more walk-in points. By mistake I hit one." On December 4 I hunted Corky for a couple of hours then gave her young daughter Nick her first turn in a grouse woods. That was fifteen years ago.

This autumn, mother Chip and aunt P.D. will have to share the coverts with a new pretender. Her youthful presence will keep all of us young. And considering an event that occurred when the 1996 puppies first struggled to stand on their feet, there just might be work for all of us.

That drumming on the dark snowy March night followed by his dawn salutes, which persisted through a terribly depressing cold, wet April and early May, was for a good cause. When the puppies were ten days old my wife was picking fiddlehead ferns in the woods next to the kennel. As she reached to pluck one from a clump alongside a mossy, fallen log, a grouse exploded at her feet frightening the life out of her. There were ten eggs. When the pups were three weeks old the chicks hatched. The following weekend the temperature went below freezing, the wind came from the north and an inch of snow blanketed the wildflowers. The tiny grouse huddled under their mother. We wish them well.

We have left the nose prints on the window glass and storm door as a tribute from one of my favorite nut cases to their father.

Gone But Not Forgotten

by Bill McClure

Grouse Alley is gone now, but if I were inclined to use the overused I would call it a classic partridge cover. But it also gave us exciting woodcock shooting, a few snipe, and the odd chance at a teal. Grouse Alley was my favorite, and we were in our prime together.

Kip, a Brittany and one of my best gun dogs, reached the apex of her powers at Grouse Alley, and together we shared the breathtaking spell of wild birds in wild land. From its discovery until my last hunt there, the covert maintained its reputation for making grouse.

I found this place both by accident and design. One morning, while shooting a few miles away, I met some school children walking along a concession road that my dog and I had come out to. They asked me about the dog and what I was looking for. When I told them partridge, I asked if they ever saw any. "Yes," they replied. "Along the old road that led from the village back into the McGuigan place." One of the children described with wide eyes how the birds frightened them with their noisy flushes. I asked directions, consulted my topographical map, and drove to the west end, where I found a rutted, muddy trail leading into the forest. In the distance I could see a small hill.

With care and trepidation I was able to ease my truck to the base of the hill where I found a pull-off by an unused gravel pit. A grouse flushed when I got out of the vehicle! At the top of the grade the long, lovely road allowance confirmed the children's observation. We moved eleven grouse in less than a mile. The escapees, and there were many, flushed away from the trail, back south from whence they came. Their evacuation was simple and carefully thought out. When pointed between the road and cedar fence, the grouse waited until I was in the shallow ditch en route to the dog, then sprung low and winged across the field to safety. Others exhibited Victoria Cross bravery by busting out immediately to streak down the open lane.

But there weren't that many Victoria Cross grouse, and commonly Kip would find her birds along the broad road allowance, tight to the cedar rails. Hunting alone made a clear shot all but impossible except for the occasional break in the cover or a fortuitous set of circumstances. Over the years, three of these lucky breaks were on pairs that jumped together, presenting rarely encountered opportunities for a true double. But those were the days when my youthful quick draw resulted in a hasty first shot. I was lucky to get the second bird each time. Many times, two, three, four, or more grouse that had been enjoying a meal of fallen grapes and greens departed in sequence, leaving Kip and me riveted in the ensuing silence.

There were special places that you could count on. Ahead, Kip's bell would change cadence as she slowed near the spring-fed pool that once watered cattle. There was often a woodcock in the young aspen. Farther down, an old log fence came in from the right, and at its junction with the lane, grapevines intertwined with apple and cedar trees. Here Kip pointed on principle, and usually her principles were correct. Sometimes the grouse flushed like a wraith behind the cedar, and just as often it took off behind me, eliciting one of those ungraceful gunner's pirouettes that culminate in a modified Scottish reel.

Next came a three-hundred-yard stretch where the vines, berries, and brush created a canopy like a giant tunnel on the south side. In the woods beyond, little clearings, grassy glades, alders, and young poplar reached back for hundreds of yards. Birds flew or walked out to take dessert under the tunnel. Kip learned to penetrate its walls and work the outside while I stayed on the path. If we were lucky, the bird got sandwiched between us, sprang up, and topped the cover. There were many taken in this run. All the breathless action came to a conclusion when we reached an open field, with the village in the distance across the flat farmland.

Then the real shooting began. Here we left the road and headed south into young poplar, alder, and sandy, slightly undulating landscape that stretched for almost two miles. After a few sorties I developed a route, unmarked but understood in the mind of dog and man. First came the poplar groves with willow and alder along the edges. Invariably there were two or three grouse there, and at the right time in October, a fall of woodcock. This was truly a flight cover, which early in the month would show a bird or two and a week later a couple of dozen—sometimes more. It is the only place I have ever seen a Brittany shaken to her pads by the enormity of the problems confronted. It is also the covert where woodcock jumped in ones and twos when Kip and I were in the process of crawling through the fence. It was here that Kip virtually gave up trying to handle her birds cleanly. There was so much scent and so many touchy woodcock that every twenty steps sent another on its way. She knew it was hopeless. In this corner I learned what a real shooting slump is like, and in the years to come I carried another double gun in the truck in case the one I cradled let me down. Twice I had to go for the reserves. Isn't psychology wonderful?

Wonderful, too, was what came after the timberdoodle corner. An old cow path breached a willow swale for several hundred yards, giving us a few moments of relief from the action, and ended at a low-lying, seven-acre clearing. In wet autumns there were puddles between the hummocks and an occasional snipe. The edges were decorated with conifer clumps, willow, and alder, but thirty yards inside, the ground rose slightly into the more characteristic sandy knolls. A woodcock find or two was possible along the border, and a grouse point was likely among the grassy knolls. One that I remember took place when I was shooting over Kip's grandson, Prince, in his second season. I was accompanied by a friend who was out of shape from too many cigarettes and too much whiskey. When we came to the clearing, Prince cruised the edges, reaching wide and deep to the right, then crossed the wetlands and began to work down the left side toward me. My pal was bringing up the rear. The bell stopped, and I hastened to the find to handle Prince on his bird. I spied him gazing proudly at a great cock grouse perched on a mossy log. Both participants were tense and in their own way hopeful. I waited as long as I dared, and with my oxygen-starved companion in view but out of range, the bird began that telltale nodding indicating imminent flight. At the moment of his departure

I fired, Prince retrieved, and my huffing-and-puffing pal shouted, "You grassed him, you grassed him."

From there we would swing south, following an old wire fence among mixed hardwoods, small clearings, alder, willow, and brush. On a sunny afternoon we might surprise a grouse dusting on a sandy hummock.

Just ahead was the crown jewel. In early October, the mature hardwood patch was spectacular, ablaze against a clear blue sky. I always paused here, sometimes photographing the scarlet maples and sitting on the soft, mossy ground. On a still morning we could hear a red maple leaf fall twenty yards away. Just down the incline was what we had come for.

On the far edge of the hardwood was the portion of the covert from which the whole place got its name. This was Grouse Alley. With the red maples on the knoll as background, a long run of alder curved around the base of the hill. Between the alders and the half-grown poplar and ash in the lowland was a wide gap in the forest. For reasons that still escape me—but were obviously known to the grouse—the alder run always held birds, and the excitement they generated gave the covert its name. On reflection, I don't remember ever having taken many from this place, but the action was superb. Among the alders there were two old, fruit-bearing apple trees, and they might have accounted for the attraction; except in years when their apples were scarce, our friends the grouse were still there. When pointed, their inclination was to careen through the brush and cross the alley at full speed. Because of the precariousness of their location, there was usually a little footwork before liftoff. Once, after a lengthy flushing attempt, a grouse rose at the very end of the run, and I took it cleanly over the opening. Kip was at least sixty yards behind me, and I had to go back to release her from her position of steadiness, then both of us had to return and look for the bird.

After Grouse Alley there were two options: We could continue south, past two woodland ponds to a woods road that bisected a swale ending at cultivated fields. Or, we could turn west, traversing a wild land of conifer clumps, small wetlands, alder patches, and sandy knolls. Some of the grouse work I witnessed on this latter stretch is part of precious memory never to be surpassed. The birds were found on the knolls that were encircled by alder. One very frosty October morn, I started searching for Kip, whose bell had stilled far ahead. Minutes went by until at last I spied a flash of white on an open knoll. Her breath was condensing in the air, and as I passed her the quarry shot from the alders, giving me an easy chance from my position on the slight rise. One other year she pointed a grouse in a willow clump, I made a lucky shot, and during the retrieve Kip pointed another bird with the first one securely in her mouth. I have not seen that since. Always pragmatic, Kip put the first grouse down to go for the second.

After the knolls there was almost an hour to go unless we chose any one of half a dozen alluring detours. In the last two hundred yards we had to shoot our way to the truck through apple trees at the edge of a cedar thicket, with grapevines in the corner and a dense, fruit-laden hedge that led to the road. Often there would be a couple of birds beside the vehicle, but we were too tired.

These pleasant rambles went on for four generations of gun dogs. In the early season, I would take one Brittany out after work and be home at dark. Always, I chose carefully the dog that I would start at Grouse Alley. The young and excitable could take only a small helping of the whole, while the mature were prepared for field competition among the hummocks.

It all ended gradually. The gravel pit was reopened and a good road built. One house went up, then another followed. To the east, the village crept to the woodcock corner. Someone built in the alders. More houses appeared. A developer gave the place a name.

In the seventies, my young son would take his favorite Brittany, Corky, and his Winchester twenty-gauge single to Grouse Alley after school. Back at dark he would report astonishing action at The Tunnel. There are two of us who will never forget its real name. We had the best of it.

TOM HENNESSEY was born and raised in Bangor, Maine. Self-taught in art, he was named the Atlantic Salmon Federation's first "Artist of the Year" in 1977, and he repeated in 1978. Nine years later, he was named the federation's 40th Anniversary Artist of the Year. He also was one of thirty artists selected from the United States, Canada, and England to be represented in Canada Ducks Unlimited's "Portfolio of Waterfowl of North America."

The auctioning of his original paintings and prints has raised substantial amounts of money for organizations such as Ducks Unlimited, Trout Unlimited, The Atlantic Salmon Federation, and other conservation organizations.

Tom Hennessey's work is represented in many of the finest private, public, and corporate collections of sporting art. His illustrations have appeared in major outdoor magazines and books on hunting and fishing.

In addition to painting, he writes and illustrates an outdoor feature column for the *Bangor Daily News* and is the author-illustrator of two books: *Feather 'n Fins*, which was published jointly by the National Sporting Fraternity and Bangor Publishing Company; and *Handy to Home*, published by Down East Books.

Tom is a lifelong sportsman who ties his own flies, trains his own dogs, and tries to convince his wife, Nancy, that he must constantly gather background material for his painting and writing. *A Monument to Misty* was originally published in the *Bangor Daily News*, on November 16, 1996. It also appears in Tom's latest book, *Handy to Home*.

A Monument to Misty

by Tom Hennessey

Maybe you know what I mean when I say old bird covers remind me of abandoned cemeteries found way back in the hills. Surely you've discovered one or two in your time: moss-mantled stones grown over with briars and hardhack bush and cluttered with the bones of biomass.

The stone walls that stumble through old covers, of course, are not inscribed with names to read and possibly recognize. Yet, those familiar tangles of alder and poplar "grown up and gone by," as we say, are grand monuments to great dogs whose names are etched forever in our minds. Accordingly, I stop by an old cover every now and then and pay my respects to "Misty."

Oddly enough, the birdy Brittany spaniel came into my life through a stroke of fisherman's luck: On a June morning in 1961, Frank Gilley and I were fly fishing for striped bass in the Bangor Salmon Pool. Between strikes, we hooked onto the subject of bird dogs. Frank was feeding four "feather hounds" at the time. I, however, was dogless because my hunting partner of fourteen years, a springer spaniel named "Snooky," had flushed her last bird the previous fall.

"Y'know, I've got a Brittany you might be interested in," Frank offered. "I've got too many dogs now, and, besides, she killed a couple of my turkeys. She's about two years old and has a lot of potential. If you want her, you can have her." Shortly thereafter, we set a course for Frank's "Tip-Top Farm" on Copeland Hill.

When Misty burst from the kennel, her bobbed tail was a blur as she bounded toward me smiling, sneezing, and wiggling for all she was worth. Then and there the beautifully marked liver-and-white Brittany owned me. Typically spaniel, Misty was gentle, friendly, and full of hunting instinct, which she displayed in short order.

Our first stop after leaving Frank's place was Ring's gravel pit on the Field's Pond Road. At that time, pheasants occupied the sprawling fields, acres of feed-corn, and brushy hedgerows bordering the pond. In a field rimmed with alders, Misty began making game almost immediately. Seconds later, she locked into a solid point. And so did I, mesmerized by the magic of a pointing dog—mine—paralyzed with bird scent. When I came to my senses and walked in ahead of her, a hen pheasant flushed and flew toward the swale edging the pond. So began twelve years of bird hunting the likes of which I'll never see again.

Because I was working nights in the *Bangor Daily News*'s composing room, Misty and I hunted nearly every day of bird season, regardless of weather. Now, if you were wearing bibs instead of shooting vests back in the '60s, believe me when I say birds, particularly woodcock, were plentiful then. And covers were close by. Seldom did I hunt more than fifteen miles or so from Bangor, where I lived at the time, and seldom did I return home without a mixed bag of woodcock and partridge. It seemed that every edge and corner of cover held birds.

Simply put, hunting with Misty was pure pleasure. She

worked close, handled easily, had a full-choke nose, was stiff as starch on point, and retrieved naturally. She once swam to fetch a black duck I shot after it flushed from a beaver flowage in Glenburn.

To this day, I have never hung a bell on a dog with more heart and desire, and I've owned a few. Misty would barge out of the dog box in late afternoon with as much enthusiasm as she did when the covers were fuzzy with frost. One morning, after Frank Gilley and I had bagged a double limit of woodcock over her, the now-retired orthodontist praised the hard-hunting spaniel: "Misty, old girl, you sure know your business. I should have spent more time with you."

Frank usually hunted behind setters and pointers. In recent years, however, he followed the bell of a Brittany named "Andy." Maybe the veteran sportsman saw something in Misty. And maybe that something moved him to say this fall—the first time he was dogless in more than fifty years—"Come springtime I think I'll start looking for a Brittany spaniel."

Time, of course, is a tyrant. Eventually, the years took their toll on the little dog that so graciously taught me everything she knew about birds. By then, however, I had put a collar on an English pointer pup named "Jake." Naturally, the newcomer provided Misty a well-earned rest, but she didn't appreciate it in the least. Although she ached with the infirmities of old age, her heart still yearned for what was her life and love.

It was springtime—June, in fact, the same month she came bounding into my life—when Misty went to sleep in my arms. Admittedly, on the way to the veterinarian's office, I stopped twice while showers passed and she lifted her head to look at me with cataract-clouded eyes that, I swear, were saying she understood. Don't ever let anyone tell you a dog doesn't know. They do.

Unfortunately, the veterinarian's facilities didn't include a crematory. Therefore, I had to bury Misty. I laid her to rest, with her bell beside her, in the last cover we hunted. I kept her collar, of course, which now hangs beneath one of her pictures in my den. Every now and then, usually on my way to or from new gunning grounds, I stop by that old cover—that snarled and tangled monument— just to whistle up the image of Misty and memories of the grand times and great hunting we shared.

Now you know what I mean when I say old covers remind me of abandoned cemeteries found way back in the hills.

DAVID BOOKS currently lives and works in Helena, Montana. A transplant from the Midwest, he received a B.S. degree in forestry from the University of Minnesota in 1965, followed by a Master of Forestry from Yale University the next year. Prior to moving to Montana, he worked seven years for the U.S. Forest Service in St. Paul, Minnesota. Since 1978 he has been the editor of *Montana Outdoors,* the bimonthly magazine of the Montana Department of Fish, Wildlife & Parks.

Dave has written over a hundred stories, articles, and book reviews for such publications as *Pointing Dog Journal, Gun Dog, Wing & Shot, Gray's Sporting Journal, Field & Stream,* and *The Drummer.*

He is an avid upland hunter and has pursued birds in most of the states in the Northwest and many of those in the Midwest. He has owned and shot over Brittanys since 1977. His current dog, eight-year-old Groucho, was sired by Shoe—the Brittany that Ben Williams writes about in "The Dog That No One Wanted." "Meat Dog" was originally published in *Pointing Dog Journal,* July/August 1993.

Meat Dog

by David Books

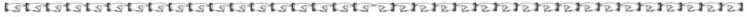

Some people call them meat dogs. I've done it myself a time or two. They're the blue-collar workers of the pointing-dog world, the unsung heroes who bring back the birds week after week. You don't see them posed with silver cups on the pages of *The American Field,* and their pedigrees don't run too heavily to field-trial champions. But you do see them in lots of slightly out-of-focus snapshots, posed proudly with pheasants or doves, grouse or woodcock, quail or chukars—it makes no difference to these four-legged hunting machines.

If they could talk, they'd probably just shrug and say, "Aw, shucks, birds is birds." True, it may take them a few days to adapt to unfamiliar country, and they're not likely to handle a new species of game bird as well as the local pros. But whether it's a milo field in Nebraska, a sagebrush flat in Montana, an alder run in Vermont, a chukar slope in Idaho, or a quail thicket in Missouri, they'll produce birds in their steady, dependable way.

They're not flashy, these meat dogs, but what they lack in famous bloodlines they more than make up in brains, heart, and desire. Come to think of it, they deserve better than to be called meat dogs. They're the best all-around athletes in the gun-dog game.

Maybe, like me, you've been lucky enough to own one. Yours may be a long-whiskered drahthaar that specializes in chukars but doesn't mind retrieving a duck now and then. Or a rangy English setter that has an advanced degree in pinning ruffed grouse but does just fine on quail or Huns. Maybe you have a sleek little vizsla that can spot a woodcock covert from the car seat but knows how to play cat and mouse with wily rooster pheasants.

Mine was a barrel-chested Brittany named Chief, who led me up mountains, across prairies, and through brush tangles for a decade and a half. My hunting partner, who wouldn't know a good-looking bird dog if it bit him on the leg, once described him as "kind of a beer keg on spindles." Maybe he did look a little like that when he was wet, but at least he didn't fancy himself too good to swim a creek to retrieve a pheasant on the other side. Besides, as I pointedly observed, Chief wasn't the only one in our party who resembled a beer keg on spindles.

Okay, I'll admit he wasn't perfect—like most bird dogs, he had his quirks and flaws. There was that time in Nebraska when I left him in the car with the birds while I stopped for dinner, and he helped himself to one or two. And, like all Brittanys, he loved to roll in things long departed from this Earth—the longer departed, the better. Then there was his belief that skunks were just striped house cats that could be chased if given the right encouragement. He wasn't bent on violence—just on having fun—but they didn't know that. So, they always anointed him in essence of polecat, an indignity that didn't seem to bother him much—or affect his hunting ability, for that matter. Me it bothered considerably, so we did a lot of driving with the autumn breeze whistling through the windows of my old Ford van.

We covered thousands of miles together over the years, chasing birds from the Saskatchewan prairie to the Arizona desert, and from the Wisconsin northwoods to the Snake River rimrocks. Along the way there were adventures with rattlesnakes, porcupines, feral cats, rabbits, coyotes, skunks, turtles, raccoons, and Chesapeake Bay retrievers. Some of these he pointed, some he bit, and some bit him—on a few memorable occasions, all of the above. He weathered the cuts, bumps, and bruises of a bird dog's life with typical Brittany stoicism—the only thing he couldn't stand was being left in the car when there was hunting to be done.

I didn't keep track of all the birds he pointed, but it was a great many. I started out with the idea that we might get around to hunting all the upland game birds in the continental United States, as Charley Waterman does with his Brittany named Kelly. We didn't quite make it, but we came close. We got them all except ptarmigan and valley quail.

What do you remember most after fifteen years of following one bird dog? If you're like me, it's the times his crazy antics made you laugh—like the way he "moonwalked" the first time you put boots on him. It's the hidden corners you explored together—the old homestead that always held a covey of Huns, the secret spring on a bone-dry chukar slope, and the abandoned pasture stiff with woodcock when the flight is in. It's the bird hunter's road you shared—hunting rigs, leaky tents, campfires, and small-town motels where the signs say "Hunters Welcome."

"He's steady as a rock," I told my partner, although secretly I wasn't sure. He'd done well in training, but this was the real thing, the opening of the Montana sage grouse season. He might have been steady, too, if it hadn't been for the jackrabbit that flushed under his nose just as we stepped into the sagebrush. Like the Roadrunner and his nemesis, Wile E. Coyote, the rabbit and the Brittany buzzed up, through, down, and around the sagebrush patch, and everywhere along their route sage grouse erupted like big brown beach balls. At some point my partner and I lost our heads and charged into the fray, running in all directions at once and screaming at the runaway Brittany. The rodeo went on for quite a while, and when the dust settled we had bagged exactly one unlucky sage grouse from a flock of about thirty.

He'd been on point for some time when I found him, trembling and bug-eyed, beneath the live oak trees along the Mexican border. I squared my shoulders and walked in front of him to flush the birds, mentally chalking up my first double on Mearns quail. In my mind's eye I saw a classic hunting pose, a scene fit to grace the canvas of a Lassell Ripley or a Robert Abbett. It turned out to be more like an Abbott and Costello. He broke when the birds came buzzing from the switchgrass and charged hell-bent after them. I don't think he tried to knock me down on purpose, but Brittany logic apparently holds that the shortest distance to a fallen bird is a straight line, and I must have been in the way. Having a chubby little Brittany barrel into the back of your legs just when you're drawing a bead on a departing covey is not conducive to good marksmanship; I shot ten feet high and three feet to the left. Chief looked a little sheepish, and for a time I wondered about his eyesight, but I think it was just a case of frazzled nerves.

〰

The bobwhites in Nebraska held tighter than the Huns I was used to back in Montana, and the explosive covey rises had a distinctly unsettling effect. I usually panicked and shot too fast.

I did better on the singles. Late one afternoon we scattered a covey at the edge of a woodlot, and I shot several birds over Chief's points. The bird I remember best was the one that flew into the woods, dodging through the tree limbs like a miniature ruffed grouse. I thought I saw it flinch at my shot, but it kept going, slanting downward out of sight in the thick stuff. The sky was getting dark, and I didn't think I had much chance of finding the bird, but I followed its line of flight, telling the dog to "Hunt dead; hunt dead." Some time later, as I was staring forlornly at the ground trying to conjure up a dead quail from the mottled pattern of twigs and oak leaves, I sensed that I was being watched. I turned around to see Chief waiting for me to take the pretty cock bird from him.

〰

High above Brownlee Reservoir on the Idaho side of the Snake River, I watched him stop on a rock outcrop, test the breeze wafting up from the valley below, and stare hard down the slope. He could have been admiring the view, but I knew better. There were chukars down there somewhere, probably in that little rock slide just below the blood-red sumac bushes.

I began picking my way downslope, trying not to dislodge rocks, trying not to slip and fall, trying not to make too much noise, trying not to . . . *Whirrrrr* . . . *Bang!* The last bird in the covey, hit poorly, fluttered and tumbled far down the hill and out of sight. Chief charged after it and disappeared. By the time I made my way to a place where I could see out over the slope below, the dog was nowhere in sight. I began to worry, wondering if he had taken a spill and hurt himself. Just as I was about to go down the hill and start searching, he emerged from behind a rockpile far below, looked up at me, then ran back and disappeared behind the rocks again. When I finally slipped and slid my way down there, I found him pointing patiently into a crevice in the rocks. I reached in and pulled out the wounded chukar.

Hidden in some mesquite trees, we sat shivering as the winter sun began to set on Arizona's San Rafael Valley. Only about ten more minutes of daylight, and not a dove in sight. Suddenly, wings whistled, and half the doves in Santa Cruz County converged on our little waterhole. Three of us fired, reloaded, fired again, and then it was quiet. The sun dropped below the horizon, signaling the end of legal shooting time.

With Chief's help, we retrieved the doves, counted, argued, and counted again. One dove short. Or were we? No longer sure, we picked up empty shells, camp stools, pop cans, and headed for the truck. Somewhere along the way, we lost track of Chief; back at the vehicle I called for him apprehensively. When he appeared, a white speck growing larger in the gathering dusk, he had the missing mourning dove in his mouth.

He'd been naturally soft-mouthed as a pup, but after a few years of wrestling with sharp-spurred Montana roosters he began to approach his retrieving chores with flashing teeth. I decided I'd better do something unless I wanted a steady diet of pheasant burger. So I did some yard training with pigeons, teaching him to lighten his grip when I'd tell him "Easy." I drew the word out in two long syllables: "Eeee-zzyy." It worked pretty well until the day I knocked down a rooster that ran and hid under a brushpile. Chief crawled in behind it and, after a lot of snuffling, snorting, digging, and scratching, backed out with the bird in his mouth. He looked excited and had a determined set to his jaws, so I crooned "Eeee-zzyy" as he came toward me with the bird. By the time I finished the second syllable, he had relaxed his grip considerably—too much, I guess, because the pheasant flew out of his mouth and lumbered away toward the nearest patch of brush. I shot the bird again, this time downing it for good. I thought I detected a hint of a smile on Chief's face when he brought it back the second time.

He was getting on in years by the time we headed east to Wisconsin, to revisit the grouse woods I had hunted as a boy. We arrived at the bridge on Fisher River early one October morning, just as the sun was lighting the treetops with crimson, orange, and yellow. I poured the last cup of coffee from the thermos and relaxed as the melting frost unlocked the aroma of decaying hardwood leaves.

I'd like to say Chief handled the skittish ruffed grouse like a pro, but dogs accustomed to ranging a couple of hundred yards on the prairie in search of Huns or sharptails don't convert to ruffed grouse specialists overnight. Still, he quickly learned to shorten his range in the thick cover and to put on his brakes at the first hint of grouse scent.

We'd hunted the better part of an hour when his bell went silent near the river, under the thornapple trees. I circled toward the bank, thinking that the bird might be pinned near the water's edge. I had a clear shot when it topped the thornapples and flew out over the narrow channel, and I heard it hit the water with a splash. Chief came back a few minutes later, dripping water, the ruffed grouse in his mouth.

I sat for a time on a pine log in a little clearing, soaking up the sun. Chief rolled and sneezed in the frost-killed bracken—his way of drying off. A gray squirrel scolded from a far-off hardwood ridge; the dark waters of the Fisher talked softly among smooth, round stones. When I shut my eyes and listened, I could hear the voices of old hunting pals calling dogs whose names I hadn't heard in thirty years.

The out-of-the-way corner of Emil's central-Wisconsin farm was woodcock heaven. A purling, tea-colored stream wandered languidly among the hardwoods. When I saw the white splotches the size of half-dollars dappling the fallen leaves and dark humus, I gripped the twenty-gauge a little tighter. Chief ran right past the first 'cock, paying no attention as it twittered up through the alder branches. I cussed and "Whoaed" him. He perked up his ears when he smelled the next one, hesitated, then flushed it. This time, in defiance of all dog-training logic, I shot the bird. Hell, I figured, he's eleven years old, not a young dog just learning his trade. He ran over to it, sniffed, and looked at me. "Woodcock!" I said dumbly, not knowing what else to say. I guess he understood, because he pointed the next six timberdoodles in a row.

It was late on a December day when I drove past the lane leading to the abandoned homestead. Bone-tired and more than a little discouraged, I'd spent the last weekend of the Montana upland bird season chasing pheasants with Chief's half-sister, Sally. Despite our best efforts, we had managed only two roosters and a couple of Hungarian partridge in two days of busting the brush. I was on my way to town for a cup of coffee before tackling the ninety-mile drive home when I made the mistake of looking back at the dog crates in the rear of the van. My eyes met the accusing stare of a fifteen-year-old Brittany who'd hardly been out of the car in the past two days. He couldn't know, as I did, that his arthritic hips were no match for the fields of waist-high cover where the pheasants were holed up.

But I couldn't stand those eyes, so I stopped, turned around, and drove back to the lane I'd passed a moment earlier. I hadn't hunted the homestead at all that year; in early fall it's a prime place for rattlesnakes, and I hadn't wanted to risk an encounter. But this late there'd be no snakes, and with luck we might catch a covey of Huns feeding in the wheat stubble or going to roost among the weeds and rusty machinery.

Once out of the van, Chief shuffled along stiffly, stumbling at obstacles he would have flown over a few years before. I began to wonder if I was wrong for putting an almost-deaf, wheezing old warrior in the field—no matter how much he wanted to go—but there was no turning back now. We'd try the easier going of the stubble first, then, if he still had the legs, the shelterbelt nearby.

When he seemed to catch a whiff of scent halfway down the wheat strip, my boots felt five pounds lighter, and when he went on point a minute later the aches and pains of a long day suddenly evaporated. The covey rose in a chirping, clattering rush, and when the few seconds of neural riot we call wingshooting were over, two Huns lay kicking on the ground.

Chief ran to retrieve the nearest bird, but his rear legs buckled as he lunged to catch it. I didn't know whether to laugh or cry at the sight of my old bird dog sprawled on the ground, sides heaving, the Hun pinned beneath his paws. We rested a long time, watching the sun wash the prairie with waves of orange and gold, then made our way back to the van.

I didn't know then that this would be Chief's last bird

hunt, but I suppose deep down I suspected as much. Fifteen years is a long life for a hunting dog. He's gone now—I hope to a place where the birds always hold and the skunks all run like house cats. But in my mind I'll always see him under the live oaks along the Mexican border, high on a chukar slope above the Snake, or beneath the shadow of the Montana Rockies, a gritty little meat dog, pointing to the birds.

STEVE SAVAGE resides with his wife and family in Woods Cross, Utah. He has hunted pheasants in that state and in Idaho for the past twenty years. A self-proclaimed outdoor enthusiast, Steve says he spends every spare minute in Utah's Wasatch Mountains, fly-fishing for trout and pursuing deer, elk, grouse, and pheasant.

He works as the assistant director of communications at Westminster College in Salt Lake City and previously served as an information technician for Utah's Division of Wildlife Resources. For Steve, writing hunting stories is a hobby.

A December Hunt was originally published in the *American Brittany*, November 1998.

A December Hunt

by Steve Savage

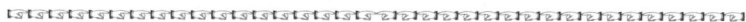

I fell in love with her the day I saw her. I had to hope she would hunt because her personality would not let me leave her to be bought by another. I had never met a young dog that showed such gentle affection as she did.

When I first approached Taz, she was timid and acted a little nervous about having a stranger confront her. While I stood by, she inched up close enough to touch my shin with her paw and to smell my boot. I looked down at her, and she stared at me with her sparkling orange-brown eyes. Without taking her eyes off me, she licked her little pink nose and waited patiently for my acknowledgment. She crouched down, almost lying on the ground, and started to smell my hand as I reached down to pet her.

I stroked her coat, and she became very excited. Her docked tail moved back and forth quickly, expressing happiness that I had accepted her.

The owner of the shy, gentle pup was well known in the area for his German shorthairs. He had picked the Brit up as a trade. He talked about the dog as he stood with his hands in his pockets, looking down at the ground and lightly kicking a small rock. "She has a great nose—that's why I got her—but like a lot of young dogs, she'll need to be worked up on her retrieving."

I'd had a Brittany before and was extremely impressed with that dog's intelligence and the ease with which he accepted training. With that in mind, and with little hesitation, I bought the little Brit called Taz.

I went to the store and purchased a medium-sized paint roller to help her with retrieving. Over the years I've found that because of their size, texture, and weight, these rollers are easier for a young dog to handle than most regular training dummies. (They're less expensive, too.) After placing the roller in her mouth, I'd have her carry it as she walked by my side. When she finally got used to holding it, I would command her to stay as I walked away from her. After moving about twenty feet, I would stop, then call her, and finally take the roller from her. We practiced the process repeatedly until it became habit. I then began throwing conventional dummies for her. She would sit patiently awaiting my release command, then take off like a flash after the dummy. It didn't take long for Taz to develop good retrieving skills.

When we started hunting, the first thing I noticed was her great athleticism, and she has excelled in that department ever since. Looking at her size, you'd think she would have a difficult time moving through heavy brush, but it doesn't stop her. She aggressively attacks cover that most dogs shy away from. Taz leaps gracefully, like an equestrian competitor jumping gates, clearing high sage as she hunts—never tiring, leaving no ground untouched.

With each bird I shot over her, retrieving became a game she loved to play even more. At the flush, she would watch with anticipation until the pheasant or grouse fell to the ground. At my command she would bound forward, then gently adjust the bird in her mouth, making sure she had a good grip. She'd strut back to me with her head held high and what always looked like a smile on her face.

Though Taz was soon retrieving much like an old-time pro, I didn't know how she would react to a downed bird in water or to a situation where she'd have to cross water to make the retrieve on land. Because I had no water to practice on and since Brittanys aren't natural water dogs like Labradors, I wondered how she would do. She had never experienced water with the exception of a bath here and there, so we spent most of our time chasing birds along fence lines and overgrown ditches, staying clear of the prime hunting along canal banks.

It was a cool December morning when Taz got her chance at the water. My wife, my dog, and I worked a field blanketed with frost-covered sagebrush and grass. The sun made the place look like a crystal gallery. The chilly, brisk wind blew directly into our faces, which made it easier for the dog to pick up scent. A fifteen-foot-wide, three-hundred-yard-long irrigation canal bordered the large field on its north side.

I commanded Taz to hunt in the sagebrush away from the canal. She covered a large area as she leaped and wove her way back and forth in front of us. Faced with the difficulty of flying in a stiff wind, the pheasants ran on the ground more than usual, making it difficult for Taz to hold them. After picking up one bird's scent, she worked hard on getting it to sit tight. But the pheasant kept moving and ran toward the water. We followed the dog as she pinned the bird between her and the canal's thickly covered bank. Taz froze, showing not so much as a muscle twitch.

I circled around her so as to approach her from the front. "Whoa," I said as she stood motionless, her head pointed into the outer edge of cover. I struggled through the chest-high brush to get close enough to flush the bird while still leaving myself a good opportunity to shoot.

With great anticipation and a little apprehension, I worked to get still nearer the dog. Suddenly, a large cackling rooster sprung from the bank under my feet. I quickly raised my gun, pushed the safety, and pulled the trigger. *Boom!* The pheasant dropped thirty feet away—on the other side of the canal. Taz, still standing without movement, waited for my command, then went crashing through the brush and into the water. Her body broke the glassy surface of the canal as she charged toward the far bank. It wasn't long before she was searching for her bird.

I was trapped by the high, unforgiving sagebrush but tried to work my way out so that I could help Taz find the bird. I couldn't see the rooster, but I could hear its wings flapping against the three-foot grass as it lay on the ground, wounded. Looking across the canal, I caught glimpses of a white-and-orange shape working its way through the cover toward the pheasant.

"Fetch," I shouted, "Fetch, girl!" I moved a few feet hoping to position myself so Taz could see me. In doing so, however, I lost track of her location. I called to her over and over. My wife couldn't see the dog, either. Totally frustrated and thinking that my Brittany had failed to retrieve the bird, I started yelling, "Come Taz! Come."

I was upset. All the time spent steadying her on retrieving, all the progress that we had made seemed to be slipping away. My mind raced with questions: Why didn't she retrieve the rooster? Did the water affect her in any way? Could she not make it back through the thick brush? What had happened?

I stood there confounded.

My wife questioned cautiously, "Honey, what if she's pointing another bird on the other side of the canal?"

I quickly ran several yards down the bank hoping to see where Taz had gone. As I reached a clearing, there she was, with the downed bird in her mouth, pointing another. I wasn't far from the bridge that crossed the canal, and I started running. My frustration instantly turned to excitement as I called out, "Whoa, Taz, whoa."

I hurried over the bridge and started down the canal bank toward her. Her point was the prettiest sight I'd seen in my twenty-two years of hunting. With the dead bird in her mouth, she was standing near the water on a little bald knoll surrounded by knee-deep grass. That's where the second pheasant was. I walked into the cover, the bird flushed, and my wife shot. The rooster dropped into the water a few feet from the shore. I walked up to Taz and took the first rooster, then she splashed into the canal and retrieved the second.

As the dog brought the bird to me, her sarcastic look penetrated mine as if to say, "Whoa? Whoa? Next time, tell me something I *don't* know!"

C. W. GUSEWELLE graduated in 1955 from Westminster College and joined the *Kansas City Star* that year as a general-assignment reporter. He became an editorial writer on foreign affairs in 1966 and foreign editor in 1976. A bird hunter for forty-six of his sixty-three years, he still lives in the Kansas City area, with his wife, Katie.

Besides doing newspaper reporting and commentary, Charles has had his articles and short fiction published in *Harper's, American Heritage, The Paris Review,* and many other magazines and journals. In addition, he has written six books, including the most recent, *Another Autumn: The Rufus Chronicle,* originally published in 1996 by Kansas City Star Books and currently available as a Ballantine Book.

For nearly thirteen years, from earliest puppyhood, Rufus—a bird dog—was a recurring character in Charles's thrice-weekly column in the newspaper. The Brittany's triumphs were celebrated, and his escapades and misdemeanors recorded. Readers of the column thought of this dog as their own. When Charles lost Rufus, he paid a final tribute to his beloved Brittany in his column. An amazing response followed—nearly four hundred letters from readers nationwide—and to date, the newspaper has received more than seven thousand requests for reprints.

Rufus

by C. W. Gusewelle

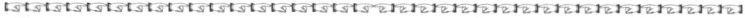

For twelve autumns Rufus and I traveled the fields together and were prodigal with our time. Almost to the last we did not consider endings.

He flew the fences. I clambered ungainly over them. He plunged boldly into the thickest, prickliest cover, while I took the easy way around the edges.

"The pup has style," a man once said, and I thought I'd won the lottery.

Rufus also had much courage and a ruling passion. If I'd ever gone at writing with a passion like that, there's no knowing what work I might have done.

"He'll live in his house outside," I told my wife when we brought him home. "He'll be a hunting machine."

That lasted until the weather cooled. Then, of course, he joined us and the old dog and the cats indoors. He slept beside the bed. But when we returned from an evening out and he met us at the door with that look of innocence, we knew there'd be a warm place on the covers where he'd trespassed.

Rufus could be devious. A sandwich unattended for a moment on the table would vanish in a gulp. Once we found him neck deep in a cake set out to cool. He lusted particularly for bagels. My wife once packed a half-dozen as provisions for a short trip to somewhere. When we opened the sack in the car, they'd been filched—all of them—with nothing else disturbed.

But those were merely vices.

His ruling devotion was to the hunt. Rufus marked the season's turning, and when the alarm sounded in the dark of a November morning, he always knew and was waiting already beside the downstairs door.

His eyes, gold when he was young, deepened to chestnut brown. A knee failed and had to be repaired. He hunted on it as eagerly as ever, not seeming to mind the price of soreness afterward. Then the cataracts began to come, but it was his nose that brought the important messages, and the nose was still keen.

I remember the first time he pointed a quail, at age seven months, as clearly as I remember the last time, which was this autumn. Nearly every man who ever walked behind him spoke of someday wanting a Rufus pup, and several have them now.

He had a dog friend, Abigail, who sometimes visited and sent him treats.

And he had hunter friends. There was Fred Kiewit, who in a year when we were out of the country drove many miles each day to take him for a run, and who saw to it that the autumn of that year was not wasted.

Fred is gone now. As is another fine man, Stuart Mitchelson, for whom Rufus pointed and brought to hand a final bird just at the mellow sundown hour of the last day Mitch and I had afield together.

And there were others—many of whom knew Rufus from the mention of him in columns over the years.

He'd been less active the last weeks, but not actually sick. Then one night, just before Christmas, we came back from dinner, and he couldn't stand. The pain was great. He had been smitten by something that, even after many days in the hospital, all the best skills of veterinary science couldn't absolutely identify or, finally, fix.

He passed his last night at home, on a pallet in the kitchen, with me beside him. He was tired and had borne enough. He had been too good a friend to hurt any longer.

In the morning, then, I dressed for the hunt—put on my boots and folded my canvas coat beside him, with the bird smell still in it. His leash was there too.

His head came up from the blanket. He'd have stood if he could. All the old excitement was in his eyes.

Dan, who'd cared for him so well from earliest puppy days, made the sad house call. The vet came to kneel with me beside him, and just as I let Rufus take the quail wing from my hand, released him to wherever it is that old gun dogs and those who've followed them finally go.

With my wife and a daughter I drove to the farm. On a day of false spring, working together under a warm sun out of season, we buried him, wrapped in the coat, facing a thicket in which he almost always found a covey.

My theology is a bit shaky, so I don't profess to know what, if anything, lies beyond the darkness. But I believe in covering all the possibilities.

So before we walked away, I looked for a long minute straight up into the cloudless deeps of that sweet spring-time sky and said—in my heart, if not actually aloud— Freddy, Mitch, I'm sending you a pretty good dog. But he isn't given, only loaned.

MICHAEL McINTOSH is one of the world's most respected gun and sporting writers. A native Iowan, he holds degrees in literature from Iowa Wesleyan College and the University of Iowa, with postgraduate study at Princeton University and UCLA. Michael and his wife, Vicky, live in the Black Hills of South Dakota.

His writing about fine guns is only one aspect of the man. He also shoots them well and is a widely respected wingshooting instructor. Michael writes the "Shooting" and "Technicana" columns for *Shooting Sportsman;* serves as senior editor for *Sporting Classics;* is a shooting columnist for *Gun Dog;* and regularly contributes to *The Double Gun Journal.*

In addition, he has written eighteen books, including *Best Guns, A.H. Fox, The Gun-Review Book, The Big-Bore Rifle, Shotguns and Shooting* and books on sporting artists Robert Abbett, David Maass, and Herb Booth.

Not Yesterday I Learned to Know the Love and *Grouse Without October* originally appeared in the March/April 1993 and January/February 1994 issues of *The Pointing Dog Journal,* respectively. These two pieces were also included in Michael's wingshooting anthology, *Traveler's Tales.*

Not Yesterday I Learned to Know the Love

by Michael McIntosh

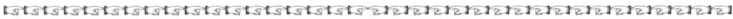

W hen he ran his dogs in field trials, my father wore a
pair of knee-high laced boots with his pantlegs
tucked inside. From my point of view, which at the time
wasn't much higher than the tops of them, they were the
most fabulous boots in the world. They meant bare, brown
fields and lean, hard-running dogs and a gun and the
promise of quail.

At first, those boots were at the center of it all, the
prime criterion, lending shape and dimension. Then Dad
showed me the real heart.

Try as I might, I cannot remember exactly when or exactly where. I was no more than six or seven, very young,
not yet a bird hunter. Dad took me along to a field trial
somewhere—eastern Iowa or western Illinois, I can't say
which. It was the first time I ever saw dogs at work in
earnest.

The fads of language unfortunately have gutted the
word of all meaning nowadays, but it was awesome, and I
was awestruck. It was a new world, beyond imagination—
a world of men and dogs and judges on horseback, and
everywhere I looked, boots just like Dad's. It was shrill sil-

ver whistles, the crackle of cornstalks underfoot, nose-twitching whiffs of horseapples faintly steaming in bright, cold air.

When the time came, Dad fetched his dog. A few men drove tall, boxy, wood-sided station wagons with dog boxes in the back, but in those days, most dogs rode in car trunks. She was waiting, eager and happy, in the cavernous space of Dad's 1948 Oldsmobile, and she seemed to tremble in an anticipation I didn't understand. Dad clipped a short leather leash to her collar, told her to heel, and we walked to the line, she on his one side, I on the other.

The other dog was taller, a big male, every muscle a-quiver. Keeping a finger hooked in her collar, Dad unsnapped the leash, rubbed her ears, and in response to some signal I didn't recognize, said simply, "Birds."

In the next instant she was gone, launched by an uncoiling of energy I could almost feel in the aftershock. Down the field she went full-stretch, sweeping a great arc. The big male was out there, too, cutting curves of his own, and we set out to follow.

I don't know how long it took. In my mind that day, there was no room for time. All I know is that Dad suddenly went off at a trot, and I remember churning through the corn stubble, thumping along as if pursuing the fading pale of grace. Then he was there again, in front of me, and he reached down and lifted me to his own height.

She was a few yards off, immobile as a monument, half bent, her forelegs crouched, tail straight out and so rigid I imagined it would twang if you brushed against it.

And Dad said, "Look at that. Did you ever see anything so beautiful?"

I had not. Not even the boots.

Nor has that same perfect beauty dimmed in the thousands of times I've seen it since.

All the principal players in that little drama are gone now—first the dogs and then Dad—leaving me, like Ishmael, to tell the tale. It's never slipped far from memory in all these years, but it came back especially clearly not long ago. I was talking with a young friend who's just discovered what bird hunting can do to your soul, and he confessed feeling confused over choosing a dog, pointer or flusher, lacking any great experience with either one. He asked what I prefer, personally, and I told him that I can imagine hunting upland birds with something other than a pointing dog—because I've done it—but I can't imagine it feeling quite complete. He wondered why, and I told him the story I've just told you.

He mulled it over for a few minutes and then asked, "Would I feel the same way?"

The most honest answer I could think of was "maybe." If you have a dog that's interested in hunting, one that's intelligently trained, one that builds upon its own experience—maybe. Maybe, too, if your expectations are realistic, if you're tolerant enough to grant the dog its imperfections, patient enough to do a lot of teaching before you expect a lot of learning, secure enough not to burden the dog with the responsibility of your own self-image—secure enough, in other words, not to see the dog as the sole arbiter of whether your hunting buddies think you're a hero or a dork.

Most of all, I told him, how you feel about hunting will shape how you feel about your dog. If action is the main appeal, a flusher might be just the ticket. But if the connection between yourself and the bird is what reaches right down into your gut and takes hold with both hands, then nothing forges that link like a dog on point. In that moment, the dog is a bridge between two worlds.

I don't know whether any of it made sense to him. It's the sort of thing everybody has to learn for himself, out of his own emotions and experience. But it set me thinking about the inward territory I've covered in the company of dogs.

To my father, "bird dog" meant English pointer, and except for a brief fling with a setter named Pudge—which happened before I was born—he was a pointer man all his hunting life. Which meant I was a pointer man, too, or a pointer boy, at least in the beginning. It also meant that what I learned of dogs early on, I learned from Cookie. She was the first friend I remember.

Almost from the moment I could walk, or so my mother's stories went, the kennel was my main destination at any given time, and I do remember climbing inside the doghouse and curling up close to that warm, hard-muscled body with the soft, floppy ears that never seemed to tire of being rubbed.

I didn't shoot my first quail over Cookie; that came as a chance encounter during a rabbit hunt. But the first pointed bird I ever shot was one of hers and so was the next and the next, until I lost count. When she grew old and eventually died, my heart broke. I believe Dad's did, too, because he didn't own another dog for a long time after.

Such was the love I discovered, and armed with all the certainty of youth, I decided early on that those who insisted gun dogs should not or could not be "pets" were conspicuously wrong. There would, in short, be no kennel dogs at my house. Not surprisingly, there were a few false starts—first a pointer, followed by a lovely, rambunctious setter named Dolly, followed by another pointer who ate a dictionary, a pair and a half of my wife's shoes and the neighbor's cat all in one afternoon, followed by a period of no dog at all, during which I began to question whether having a gun dog as housemate and constant companion was really such a bright idea after all.

About that time I accepted a teaching job in northwest Missouri, where the bird hunting was even richer and more varied than in the Iowa corn country where I'd been living, and by the following summer, doglessness was becoming burdensome. My office-mate, a linguistics professor who hadn't the slightest interest in hunting, phoned one Saturday afternoon from Illinois, where he'd gone to visit his family, and said he'd found a litter of eight-week-old Brittany pups at a flea market for $25 apiece.

At first I thought he was putting me on, finding pups at a flea market and all, but he assured me it was no joke. Rob said he was going to buy one for a pet, just because they were especially pretty, and would get one for me if I wanted it.

I'd never bought a dog sight-unseen in my life, and haven't since, but the next thing I knew, I heard myself telling him to pick the largest female in the bunch.

Two days later, Rob delivered a little orange-and-white package that stole my heart forever. One look into my new puppy's eyes and I was a goner, for her and for the breed. If you looked in an illustrated dictionary for the definition of love and sweet devotion, those eyes are what you'd find.

Ginny's training amounted mainly to come, sit, and some playful retrieving. As it turned out, that's all she needed. At four months, she pointed and held four successive single quail from my house covey. They were the first live birds she ever saw. A month later, we opened the bird season together with a nine-covey day, each one handled with great finesse, and never looked back.

Thus I came to understand that the miscues and false starts were nature's way of telling me my thinking was altogether screwed up. I suspect every young Nimrod fantasizes about owning the ultimate bird dog, the one that streaks across the fields leaving a trail of charred, smoking stubble and foxtail behind, never out of touch or control, slamming into classic points from light-speed, guided always by an infallible, full-choke nose. After the hunting, said noble beast turns into the canine equivalent of David Niven, urbane and impeccably mannered, at ease in the drawing room, laconically graceful by the fireside.

It finally dawned that my treasured images were as compatible as fire and fuel. I can't say it's impossible to find a slashing, hard-driving hunter who turns into a lounge lizard indoors—but I can say I've never seen one.

More to the point, I also realized that my approach to hunting had undergone some change. The half-blood-thirsty kid whose idea of a good day's hunt meant scouring two counties at a canter had, by his mid-twenties, come to enjoy a slower pace. He slowed even more by his mid-forties, and now, mid-forties fading behind, he is a rambling putterer—still looking for birds, but given to detours and intermissions, as apt to search for arrowheads as for likely cover, fond of sitting by streams listening to water over stones or on a fallen log to hear the woods go about its business of living.

For that kind of hunting, a big-going dog just doesn't get it. Which isn't to say I don't appreciate the hard-runner's sheer athletic drive; a few of my friends have such dogs, and I love to hunt with them—but I don't want one of my own.

This I learned from Ginny in the too-few years we had together. She died three months short of her fifth birthday, brought down by strychnine-laced peanuts that some neighborhood clod dropped into a mole run and left uncovered.

Then came Katie, a snipe-nosed genetic aberration who wore the most gorgeous coat ever grown by a dog—thick waves and curls of deep, rich cordovan red interrupted only by a narrow white blaze on her chest and two white feet. Sweet, tragic Katie, who accumulated catastrophe like other dogs pick up cockleburs; who lost the sight in one eye from some mishap I never understood; who lost her bearings and strayed off for five brutally cold December days before turning up at a farmhouse five miles from home; who lost blood from being shot by some rifle-wielding scum alive today only because I never learned his whereabouts or name; who lost more blood and much of her sense of balance after being blind-sided by a passing car; who finally lost it all dashing out of the bushes along the driveway at dusk one evening, going under the wheels of my own car.

And that was Katie, who died in my arms as I sat sobbing in a pile of sere November leaves. She was like some exotic flower struggling to bloom in a climate suited only for thorns. She haunts me still.

There was no gun dog in my house for almost two years after Katie, which is a long time to be without a key component of one's soul. But the horror of that awful night slowly faded, and I found the missing piece once more, in a suburb of St. Paul.

It was the single most beautiful litter of puppies I've ever seen, begotten by Spick's Brimstone Buster upon Sunshine Taffy II, dogs of similar bloodline whose pedigrees show a list of Field Champions and Dual Champions as long as your arm and in which eight members of the Brittany Hall of Fame appear a total of thirty-two times—the stuff of raptures, I suppose, to one more impressed by pedigrees than I.

Thanks to the help of a friend, I had first pick among the females and spent the afternoon playing with them, looking for one to give me the sign, whatever it might be, that she and I would connect in some special way.

Watching them rollick and tumble, I noticed that one in particular, a lovely little creature with an almost perfectly drawn facial mask, preferred exploring the yard to chewing on her sisters. Each in turn puppy-pointed a grouse wing, showing about equal enthusiasm. And then mine revealed herself.

The wing was tied to a fishing rod by a length of thick, white string. After a couple of play-points, the adventuresome lass who'd caught my eye earlier ignored the wing as I twitched it away from her and went for the string instead. I've always believed dogs have more capacity for reason than we think they do, and from the way she behaved, I could almost see the wheels turning inside her head: The wing always followed the string, and she couldn't catch the wing, therefore . . .

Now, I have no idea if that's why it happened the way it happened, but said pup left with me the next morning, and she's been with me ever since.

To the AKC, she is October First, which is when the woodcock season used to open here in Missouri. To me, she is variously Tober, Tobe, Toby, and frequently Dingleberry. Her passions include woodcock, anything remotely edible, quail, any bed or form of upholstered furniture, and cowflops—not necessarily in that order. Her desire to hunt is a precise match for my own, and as a retriever I'd put her against any dog of any breed, simply for the ability to find and fetch whatever falls. In the ten seasons we've been together, she has failed to find exactly one downed bird, and that one was my fault, not hers. Otherwise—dead, wounded, or merely dinged, runner or hider, in the open or the brush, in thick grass, water, snow, leaflitter, or dust—it's all the same to her. If it's down, she'll have it sooner or later.

Like many another Brittany I've known, she has a penchant for wanting to get eyeball to eyeball with the birds she points and thus doesn't always earn high marks for deftness in handling game. She's a slow worker and close, so she doesn't find as many birds as her hot-footed colleagues do. Having an alpha personality and having hunted mostly alone, she's dead certain to muscle in on another dog's point unless I'm close by, and she's as steady to flush as a six-pack of nitro.

In short, my aging friend is an imperfect gun dog. As I am an imperfect man, we get along just fine. Hard times or good times, her devotion is absolute, her love unearthly in its simple perfection. And when she shines, she shines like a bouquet of suns.

It was the last hour of the last day of the week we spend each year among the grouse and woodcock of northern Minnesota. It's always a long week in terms of knee joints and leg muscles, incomprehensibly short in the terms of my heart. As Tober and I came down the steep old farm path toward the creek, the Blazer in sight at the top of the next rise, I was thinking more about the knees and beaten-up muscles than about my heart.

Tobe was tired, too. This Minnesota gig is usually her first intensive work of the year, and she was eight then. For a half-hour or so, she'd stayed mostly at heel, by choice, but as we drew near the creek, she caught some tendril of smell she liked and slid under the fence to check it out.

From the way she vacuumed around in tight circles, it was clear that a grouse had puttered this same hillside in the recent past. Slowly, she wound a torturous upward path. I looked at the slope, thought of my aching knees, and gave her a tentative "come," more question than command. I al-

C. SMITH

ready had three birds in my vest and really didn't care if there should be a fourth. She paid no attention, working higher still in the scribbly gestures a dog makes when following the foot-scent of a grouse. One more "come" and a soft whistle got the same response, so I sighed, clambered over the fence, and followed slowly behind.

Thirty yards and about ten minutes on, she picked up the pace, and I came on edge. A moving grouse in open woods surely wasn't going to sit still for the kind of nose-to-nose point Tobe is wont to make.

Then she simply stopped.

At first I thought it was the scant remains of a cabin, twenty feet off her nose. On second look, it was just one fallen tree that happened to land on top of another. But together they formed a breastworks logical for a grouse to use as shelter—and an equally effective screen to block any shot I might have at a low flush.

How many grouse would stay put, knowing full well the fix it was in, while I struck off, gained the elevation and came in from the side? One in fifty, maybe.

I told Tobe that staying cool was the name of the game and moved off sideways. Still fearing a wild flush, I figured ten steps were all I could risk. Suddenly, I wanted that bird more than gold or salvation. A few slow yards uphill brought me to where any flush would at least be in sight, and then I moved back to intersect the invisible line from her nose to the bird, so plain you could draw it without a ruler.

It ended without drama. Five paces on, a grouse whirred up, straightaway; I caught its path in almost a throwaway gesture with the gun; it fell dead, and my dear, dear girl trotted over, picked it up, and brought it in, eyes shining.

My eyes shone, too, as I hopped stone-to-stone across the creek while Tobe splashed through, stopping for a quick drink before we tackled the last hill up the pasture.

Her shining, I suspect, was in the satisfaction of a job well done. Mine came from forty years of love lodged firmly in my throat.

Grouse Without October

by Michael McIntosh

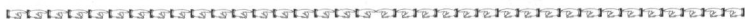

I kept hearing her bell when no bell was ringing, and caught with the corner of my eye flashes of white where nothing white was moving. Even the crackle and chop of her footfalls were there, a counter-rhythm under the sound of my own, but they ceased every time I stopped to listen.

It was odd, like an old familiar song played slightly out of tune or a once-comfortable glove with two fingers missing—faintly perverse, a level world gone the merest fraction on the slant.

After two days, I looked at Bill and said, "This just doesn't feel right."

He drew back from the long thoughts in his curling pipe smoke, knowing exactly what I meant. "Nope," he said, "sure doesn't."

We had reasons for choosing the covert we were in, and they didn't all turn on the fact that it's a reliable place to find grouse in a year when grouse are hard to find. As Bill put it when we turned down that particular gravel road, "Gibby's woods oughtta be okay for two old dogless hunters. . . ."

He was right, of course, but there's okay and then there's okay.

I don't mind being an old hunter. In fact, I enjoy my hunting days more now than I ever did when I was a young hunter—and when I was a young hunter, the world began and ended with birds and guns.

But I do mind being an old dogless hunter. I mind that very much, because the older I get, the more clearly I see that the duality I once recognized actually is a triad, bird and gun and dog, complete, indisseverable.

As I measure time, it was an extraordinary October, because for the first time in ten years the other October—the one the AKC knows as October First—didn't go with me to ramble through the Minnesota grouse coverts we love so well.

It started ten days before, with my sweet old Brittany girl sprawled unladylike flat on her back in my lap, snoring through a movie. Far as she's concerned, books and the VCR are of value only because they're tickets to uninterrupted belly-rubbing. That's when I noticed the mass, too large and indistinct to be called a lump, hovering under the skin down low inside her left hind leg. Alien topography on a familiar landscape.

Next day, Doctor Jim Wilsman tried his hand on the same place.

"Could be a hernia," he said, "or just some fatty tissue surrounding a lymph node. Feels like a hernia, though. Best have a look inside."

Monday morning, we both looked, Jim behind the scalpel and I stroking her throat while she inhaled anesthetic through a trach tube. Her tongue lolled impossibly long. She looked so vulnerable, lying there in the surgical trough. I kept my hands on her, transferring what I hoped was life and energy.

"Hernia," Jim said finally, nudging aside a wad of fat half the size of a tennis ball. I peered over his shoulder, and could see the rent in her abdominal wall.

Three layers of sutures and a few recovery hours later she was home, dopey and sore and out of sorts, sleeping heavily on the loveseat and rousing herself only for creaky trips outdoors and to her water bowl. It was a long night for me, while she slept.

She was in fine fettle the morning I left for Minnesota, ready as always and clearly worried that something was amiss. Physically, nothing was. The incision was knitting tighter by the day. I would have postponed the trip for another week, but I was committed to a magazine story on duck shooting in Canada, with grouse week to follow, I couldn't risk that tender, still-sutured belly in the brush. I left her sulky, almost outright angry.

For two weeks, she was there and not there. I could hear the faint tinkle of her little brass bell every time the wind shifted, and had to remind myself to look closely at every hit and down-arcing bird. Without realizing it, I've grown careless of marking falls, gone complacent in the knowledge that she's on the job.

At night, no immovable object occupied the exact center of the bed. No imperious morning barks summoned me to the cabin door. No need to look for an out-of-the-way turnoff for the periodic airings-out. No one to talk to for hours on the road. The world was incomplete.

Next year, I kept telling myself. Next year will be just like always. . . .

But this year my old friend Bill sat with me dogless in the woods and smoked his pipe while a thin sheen glistened on his eyes. I was temporarily dogless through a quirk, but Bill's Rosie was gone, too, really gone—sweet, silly Rosie, whose fire burned white-hot from the moment of leaving home to the moment of getting back, who rejoiced in the smell of grouse. A shattered shoulder and a needle laden with mercy took Rosie down almost at the same moment I watched Doctor Jim tie the last knot that put October well.

Hunting is an exercise in futures. Somewhere a bird is waiting, and the moment is waiting for the triad to gather. It's always ahead, like time, always waiting.

DAVID WEBB and his wife, Emma, live in what used to be a rural area of western Pennsylvania. Born in Indiana and raised in Ohio, Dave received a B.S. degree from Baldwin-Wallace College and a Master of Forestry from Duke University. He spent thirty-five years in the field of wood coatings and wood preservation, and more than thirty of his technical articles on those subjects were published. A longtime competitive target shooter Dave has written more than forty articles for *The American Rifleman, Handloader,* and *Rifle* magazines, and has contributed pieces to both *Gun Digest* and *Handloader's Digest.*

Dave Webb has bred, trained, field trialed, shown, and hunted Brittanys for some thirty years. He and Emma are now "empty-nesters" whose three sons are pursuing their own careers. However, each has a Brittany of his own, and their youngest son is actively involved in field trials. There are currently four Brittanys—Dewey, Bear, Echo, and Herb—in the Webb household.

The Eyes Have It

by David Webb

As I gently move the ball of my thumbs over his cheeks, the dog's eyes close. A moment later they open. So much trust. I cradle his head in the palm of my hands, rubbing behind his ears with my forefingers as I continue to speak in a quiet voice.

His sparkling eyes are so open, a portal into the very depth of his essence. Their centers, the irises, are almost pitch black, surrounded by a rim of golden brown. I ponder what this Brittany pup is thinking and wonder whether he thinks at all. Does he have a soul? Maybe someday I will find the answer.

What I do know is that he can't seem to get close enough to me. He wraps one leg around my forearm and rolls his head to one side and looks into my face. He stares with fixed, wide-open eyes, then turns away quickly. In just a moment he looks back again with that calm, trusting, intent expression.

In a way I am transfixed, held motionless by the pup's gaze. I dream, forming a mental image of this pup casting along a fencerow, whirling ninety degrees, freezing on his first quail point, holding for a moment, then pouncing to flush the bird. He chases, trying to catch the quail, but to no avail. Twenty or thirty yards into the pursuit, the Brit turns and comes back to me. His eyes ask: Did I do good, boss? He sure did.

A moist tongue licks my chin and brings me out of my trance. The dog's gaze is again fixed on mine. The eyes have it.

A Tiger with Attributes

by David Webb

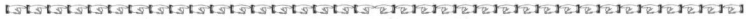

I'd like to share with you some reflections on a Brittany by the name of Tiger, or more properly Flatwood's Tiger. Even more important, I'd like to tell you about attributes and their relationship to Tiger and his progeny.

I really didn't have much association with this orange-and-roan Brittany during the years that Tiger was actively campaigned on the field trial circuit. At just about ten years of age, he was retired by his owner. Seven or eight months later he became the sire of a litter of ten puppies from one of my son's Brittanys. It seems hard to believe that this happened six years ago, but I have one of the pups from that litter—an orange-and-white male by the name of Dewey—and he just turned six this past summer.

I didn't know much about Tiger beyond his reputation. He was a field trial competitor of the highest class, and his accomplishments were well known in both his home stomping grounds—on the Brittany Central East Coast field trial circuit— and at the national level—in the Brittany Open All-Age Classic and Championship events. He pointed his birds with style and intensity. And I heard that Tiger was known for his stamina afield.

He took his first blue ribbon at the tender age of eighteen months, completing his field championship just eight months later. He went on to win or place in numerous trials. Most notable was the year 1992, when Tiger placed second in a field of sixty-nine Brittanys during the National Open All-Age Championship. Of further significance was that one of his get, Field Champion RFS Tiger's Holly, placed third in the same event.

Now let's consider the word "attribute." My dictionary defines the noun as: "1. an inherent characteristic; 2. a word ascribing a quality." In Brittany circles, it is assumed that when shopping for a new pup one should look for specific characteristics—or attributes, if you will—that are desired in a good bird dog. These include a strong desire to hunt and point birds with intensity. Biddability—the dog's willingness to respond to the trainer/handler—is also a significant attribute. Of equal importance are endurance and temperament. Plain and simple, these attributes and their "fine tuning" are what Bob Wehle has focused on over the past sixty-odd years with his Elhew line of pointers.

Since it's all but impossible to identify such characteristics in a young pup, one should look for these attributes in the dam and sire of the litter. I see Tiger's qualities every day. They are visible every time Dewey whirls and establishes a point with such intensity that he quivers; whenever he is steady to wing and watches as the bird is taken by the gun; each time he honors another gun dog's point; whenever he completes an hour-long field trial stake and still has more run to give; every time he playfully licks and paws at a young Brittany pup; whenever he puts his head on my arm and looks-up as if to say "rub my ears"; and on all those occasions when he follows me from room to room, wanting to be wherever I am.

With most of Dewey's field and show efforts behind him, there will be more time for the two of us to spend afield in pursuit of birds. I will also start thinking about my Brittany's passing along his attributes in the same manner that Tiger gave them to his offspring. Thus, the dam of the future litter will need to be from bloodlines similar to Dewey's.

With a little care and good luck, his inherited attributes can even be intensified in the next generation.

Nose Prints

by David Webb

"How can you possibly see out of these windows?" asked my better half. She had just slid into the front seat of the vehicle that my three Brittanys regard as their exclusive domain.

The reader needs to know that before my wife entered the car, I had quickly brushed all the loose, feathery, white dog hair from the seat with my orange ball cap. I just knew Emma would not want it clinging to her coat and dress slacks.

I hoped she wouldn't notice the muddy paw prints on the seat, and as I brushed away the hair, I found myself wishing that I had a wet rag. No matter—she didn't mention them. But with her next statement I regretted that I hadn't used Windex to get rid of the smudges on the glass.

"I can't believe it!" she exclaimed. "This car has gone to the dogs, and I mean it literally. What filthy windows!"

With a bit of dry humor, I responded, "But dear, you know these are nose prints. See? This one in the top right-hand corner is Dewey's. And the one over there on the bottom, next to the side window, is Bear's. Oh, here's one of Herb's in the middle of the windshield."

My wife was unimpressed. "What the devil are you talking about? Those are nothing but dirty smudges from

your dogs. You can't tell me you know which of those marks were made by which dog."

"Now wait a minute," I persisted. "A dog's nose—and especially a Brittany's nose—is just like a man's or woman's fingerprint. Each is different and has its own distinguishing characteristics. My Brittanys all have different nose prints."

"Rubbish!" said Emma. "You even have a smirk at the corner of your mouth. These are just filthy windows, and you're just making excuses for your dogs. You should have cleaned the glass before this."

Then we both laughed.

But that was the first and last time my wife rode in the "dog car." It was a good thing, because several weeks later, while I was discussing some business affairs in a local restaurant with my son, my Brittany Herb chewed the

leather covering from the steering wheel. There was no sense in scolding him; the damage was already done. I had simply spent too much time talking to Dan, and Herb had become bored. Black electrician's tape did a repair job that was just fine for the dog car.

This past year, in November, we donated this marvelous automobile to the National Kidney Foundation. The transmission was making funny noises, as were the brakes. As the tow truck rumbled down our driveway, I am absolutely sure I saw Dewey's nose print illuminated by the sunlight on the front windshield. I allowed myself a moment of regret that the new Brittany pup, Addy, wouldn't have the chance to put her signature on the windows of the dog car.

MARTHA H. GREENLEE lives in northwestern Pennsylvania with her husband, Tom, who owns and operates an Orvis retail store. She got her first Brittany in 1991 and now has a kennel full of them. Martha has hunted her dogs in the Southwest on Gambel's quail, in the Midwest on pheasants, and in the Northwest for grouse and woodcock. In addition, she competes with her Brittanys in field trials, both breeding and training her own dogs.

Martha has a Master of Fine Arts Degree from Cranbrook Academy in Michigan. She has received two Pennsylvania Council on the Arts grants and has had solo exhibitions in New York, Chicago, and San Francisco. Her work appears in numerous private and public collections.

The following story was originally published in the *American Brittany* magazine of May 1997.

The Broke Dog?

by Martha H. Greenlee

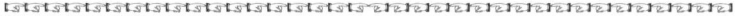

Why is a dog broke—steady to wing and shot—one minute and busting birds the next? A friend once said that a dog is stone broke when you put the stone over its grave. A bit blunt? Perhaps, but it may be accurate, too.

Take Ginger, one of my Brittanys. She started running in all-age field trials at two years old. During her first season of competition, it became evident that I could enter her in only one event per trial. She would be steady and would point beautifully on the first day, but on the second she would come unglued and usually had to be picked up.

The next year, after the spring trials, Ginger had a litter of puppies. It was late August before I made an attempt to get her ready for competition in the fall.

A warm September afternoon was the setting for the first field trial. It seemed like only a few minutes into the breakaway before Ginger found herself in the middle of a quail covey. She whirled and pointed briefly, then became airborne. Her bug-eyed expression said it all: "That wasn't just one quail, it was a smorgasbord!"

That year, pheasant season opened in Pennsylvania on November 2. Ginger was still not steady to wing and shot, but I was hopeful that shooting some pheasants over her finds would help in the training. On opening day, we hunted an older Brittany and had considerable bird work. We decided to take Ginger out for a couple of hours the next day.

The area to be hunted was a hundred-acre field with a swale in the middle. There were wide strips of tall, fallen grasses that formed big hollow mounds interspersed with rows of bushy gray dogwood, with cornfields nearby. It was excellent cover, but the ground seemed to be wet everywhere, which made the footing difficult.

While buckling Ginger's beeper collar, I slipped. She was instantly off, flying over the ground and cover. The beeper rang out. Soon she was into and working one of the grassy mounds, and the chirp of the collar changed to the point mode. In I went, kicking the grassy area. Out the far side of the mound flushed a legal hen pheasant. With one quick shot the bird was down. Ginger stood steady, looking like a million bucks. She was steady to wing and shot after all! She was, in fact, a broke dog.

Just one more bird, I thought. Ginger began working the middle of a hedgerow. Her nose was down and popping, so I knew that she had to be trailing a running bird. While I was moving quickly toward the row's end, a cock pheasant flushed and took to the air, cackling. Ginger was out of sight, but her beeper collar told me that she was still moving. As the big, gaudy bird flew across the field, I spotted Ginger in hot pursuit.

So much for my broke dog.

Fortunately, Ginger has matured since then. We've had several successful grouse seasons together and numerous productive quail hunts. In the field-trial game, Ginger has earned sixteen placements, and at the 1998 American Brittany Club National Gun Dog Championship in Ionia, Michigan, she finished third in a field of seventy-three Brittanys.

Amateur Field Champion Ginger Quill recently turned six years old. If an insatiable desire to hunt and to find birds are to be considered crimes, she is guilty as sin. When we're running a trial and that bug-eyed expression appears on her face—when the love of birds so totally overwhelms her that I know she's going to lose the handle—I've learned to pick her up and try another day.

Is Ginger a broke dog? Ask me tomorrow.

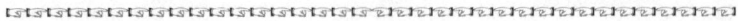

LOIS MANNON is a native of New Jersey and lives in Southampton with her husband, Bob, and their two sons, Craig and Jake. She has a B.S. degree in radiology from Thomas Jefferson University and practices her profession at the University Hospital.

Brittanys have been a recent addition to the Mannon family, the first arriving in 1995. To quote Lois, "We were afraid that when the boys went out on their own, there would be nothing to occupy the time. It only took one ornery, red-headed pointing dog to change our lives. Because of that dog, we sold our home, bought a farm, purchased two field-trial horses, and acquired two more Brittanys. I can't remember when we have had so much fun. We really enjoy watching these dogs do what they were born to do—hunt and find birds."

In Pursuit of Puppy Points, was originally published in *The Pointing Dog Journal,* March/April 1999.

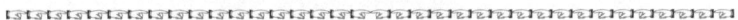

In Pursuit of
Puppy Points

by Lois J. Mannon

Admittedly, I'm new to this field-trial stuff. I'm certainly no handler, and I am at best a mediocre scout. But I can say this: Even I knew that Ruby was not a "walking-stake" puppy. We had enough trouble working her on horseback and not losing her.

But that didn't stop us. Knowing full well the extent of her running instincts, we hoped for the best and entered her in a walking stake anyway. That's the fun part about watching puppy trials—sometimes you're lucky enough to experience the flash of the true competitor to come: desire, pursuit, and maybe even a solid point. Or, you get to rescue your howling pup from the sticker vines because he jumped after some errant moth. Problem is, there's no telling which pup you're going to see from one day to the next.

Ruby was our little bit of "flash." My husband and I were convinced a first-place ribbon was finally within our reach. She was an eight-month-old Brittany with a body like a greyhound and the speed to match. Her long, leggy strides—combined with her sheer independence—made this normally tender, timid pup a surprising competitor in the field. She would scour the edges, then lock up in mid-stride, tail erect. The point would last until you started to get off your horse. Then she would bust the bird and chase. But it was all there: desire, pursuit, and point.

On the day of the trial, with the handlers on foot, the first pair of dogs was released. Frankly, I was happy to be on a horse with the rest of the gallery. When her turn came, Ruby didn't disappoint us. At the sound of the whistle, she was out and away, sucking the leaves and dust in after her, running well ahead of her bracemate. At the first objective, a hedgerow of thick bushes, she locked up and waited, glancing only once at the sorry handler breaking into a run a half-mile back. Before he could get there, she broke and was off again through the hedgerow and down along the open field. Suddenly, she was out of sight of the weary foot soldiers.

My husband turned and waved for me to scout her down. I nudged my horse into a trot and followed her trail, hoping I could turn her back up onto the course and into the judges' view. Ruby was already two farmers' fields ahead of everyone. She swung around the thick edges in a long, effortless sweep; just as I would start to get around her, she would disappear into the thickets. It was as if she was playing with me, as if she knew to go somewhere I couldn't follow her.

The brush was so dense along the edges that I couldn't get through on horseback, so I had to ride out of one field and quickly veer into the next after the dog. I was confident she couldn't get too far away, for we were approaching the lake. I was sure that when Ruby reached that obstacle, she would run out of ground and follow the shoreline back up and onto the course with everyone else.

When I reached the corner where the road met the lake, no one had seen her come up from the heavy brush. It was clear that I had to abandon my horse and look for her on foot.

I was faced with a dark, dense, triangular ravine of low branches and tight scrub pines. I didn't know how Ruby had gotten through it or in which direction she had gone. The drop into this brush was at least eight feet, but *I wanted those puppy points.* So I grabbed onto the nearest branch, lamely thinking that I could lower myself down. I went down all right, thinning out every dead branch in my way.

When I got up, I stumbled blindly through the thick cover, calling Ruby's name. I couldn't see anything. In fact, I didn't even see the lake until I stepped into it, ankle deep. Still calling up and down the shoreline, I finally heard something, a small voice from on the water yelling, "Out here!" Perhaps someone in a boat had a better vantage point and could see her on the shore.

I shaded my eyes to look toward the lake. About fifty feet away was the silhouette of a small, flat-bottomed boat. Two fishing lines were casually set in the water. The boat contained the figures of a large man and a small boy and . . . *my dog!*

Ruby had apparently swum to the boat and climbed in with them—right in the middle of the brace! She was peering over the side, and they had mercifully wrapped a towel around her shivering shoulders.

I called to her. Ruby stood rigid with her front paws on the gunwale of the boat, her ears perked. She would look at the water, then at me, then at the water. I asked the two fisherman to throw her in, but they couldn't pry her from the gunwale.

My husband heard me calling and came crashing down into the ravine with the same finesse that I had. I will always remember the look on his face when his eyes followed my pointing finger out onto the water and focused on the boat. That look was worth a thousand first places.

When his unbelieving gaze finally came back to mine, I couldn't contain myself any longer. I started laughing—so hard that my sides hurt. Of course, my husband saw no immediate humor in the situation. All he could see were his puppy points—gone fishing. He convinced the boaters to motor closer and get the dog back into the water. When she swam to us, Bob took her back onto the course and released her again.

To our surprise, Ruby took a fourth that day, and none of her placements since have ever equaled that one. Our young Brittany's performance was the highlight of everyone's weekend.

STEVEN MULAK still lives in his hometown of Chicopee, Massachusetts, close to his favorite New England coverts, where he admits to spending far too much time hunting birds. His wife, Susan, and their two daughters put up with him as best they can.

Steve has fine artistic ability, and his three books, *Brown Feathers, Pointing Dogs Made Easy,* and *Wings of Thunder,* were illustrated with his own drawings. His short stories have appeared over the past twenty years in various outdoor magazines, including *Outdoor Life, Sports Afield,* and *Gray's Sporting Journal.*

Steve trains and hunts bird dogs, has entered them in field trials, and has judged them in competition. When not in pursuit of upland birds, sketching, or writing, Steve Mulak continues his career as a marine engineer.

"One Mighty Fine Bird Dog" originally appeared in *Brown Feathers.*

One Mighty Fine Bird Dog

by Steven Mulak

I spent half my life teaching dogs to honor a point and behave like decent human beings," the Old Man said. "Now I got a friend who don't even know how to behave like a decent dog. I think maybe we don't hunt with Joe no more.

—Robert Ruark

Sandy fought the wheel as the old Chevy bounced along the gravel road, bottoming out on nearly every bump. In the backseat both bird dogs complained in low mutterings, not quite barking out loud. The car hit a particularly large pothole, and on the passenger side John's head hit the roof. *"Christmas! Slow down,* for cryin' out loud."

"Sorry." Sandy shrugged. "I'm just about moving."

"You're doing fifteen on a ten-mile-an-hour road." John pointed at the floorboard. "The pedal in the middle— that's the brake. See it down there?" Sarcasm had been an integral part of their friendship since high school. After a moment John asked, "Is the Greek still behind us?"

Sandy reached back to move his Brittany's head out of the way, then glanced in the mirror and gave an affirmative nod. George's Chrysler, with its massive hood and fenders, pitched and yawed like some ocean vessel as it labored over the rutted road behind them. The spray of water that erupted each time one of the wheels hit a pothole only added to the illusion. Through the Chrysler's visored windshield he could see Jimmy sitting on the passenger side, holding on with both hands. Most likely he was pointing out the brake pedal to George, too.

After a moment, Sandy said, "I don't think George and Jimmy are too crazy about this field trial idea, either." He referred to an earlier conversation.

"Shoot-to-kill trials are different—it'll be a good time."

"Well . . . . You know me and field trials."

John considered his reply for a moment before he spoke. "With you, I don't think your problem is so much with field trials as field *trialers*."

Sandy smiled but said nothing.

When they reached the clubhouse, he parked next to several other cars in the lot. John let the dogs out but held their collars. Both men wore rubber-bottomed pacs and had tucked their pantlegs into the tops. George pulled up next to them.

The Chrysler's door swung open. "What a miserable road. I just had the wife wash the car, too." He opened the trunk, letting two dogs out. George the Greek, as they called him, insisted in the face of criticism that the trunk of a car was the right place to transport a bird dog.

Sandy tapped at the window of the passenger side, where Jimmy sat immobile. "Are you going to get out?"

The gray-haired senior member of the group rolled the window down, affecting disbelief. "The Greek's crazier than you are—he was going to pass you back there—on *that* road!"

George patted the woodwork on the '47 Town & Country. "This baby would have done it, too—except I changed my mind at the last minute when I saw you go out of sight in that pothole."

Their four dogs, once released, raced past the clubhouse and ran to the pheasant pens beyond. Two dozen roosters flew up at their approach, only to hit the overhead netting and fall back to the ground. The two setters and the springer ran back and forth excitedly, unsure of what they were expected to do with the penned birds, but Sandy's Brittany stood back, trembling as she watched more birds than she had ever imagined.

The dogs were whistled in. His companions headed for the clubhouse, but Sandy walked with his Brittany beyond the pens, as much to see the grounds as to stretch his legs after the hour's drive. Despite the melt going on, patches of snow still clung to the north sides of the hills and in the shadows of the rock walls that crisscrossed the fields and woods. Winter-as-usual in Connecticut was a tenuous season at best: cold one week and thawing the next. The potholes in the roads gave testimony to that fact.

The Brittany had a lengthy pedigree and a formal name, both in French, but his children called the puppy Annie, and the name had stuck. As Sandy climbed the hill back to the clubhouse, an older man in a red plaid jacket crossed toward the pheasant pens. "What kind of a dog is that?" he called.

"A Brittany. I brought her back from Europe with me in 'forty-five."

"Make sure you get braced with a springer, then."

"Oh, she points just fine." By now, Sandy was used to conversations like this.

"A pointin' spaniel, eh?" The man squatted to rub the Brit's ears. Sandy noticed he held his cigarette away from the dog. "She must be quite a meat dog."

"She's been called worse—sometimes by me."

The man smiled, then stood and offered his hand. "Tom Lamica. I'll be judging today."

Sandy introduced himself and shook the man's hand. "This is quite a set-up you've got here—and that's certainly a nice touch." He indicated the pheasant pens.

The older man laughed humorlessly. "Yeah, it was a good idea during the summer, but people don't turn out for a shoot-to-kill once hunting season's over."

"Your club should get some business today: I came with three other guys, and I hear Brownie and his bunch are bringing their dogs up today."

Tom squinted through his cigarette smoke, examining Sandy closely. "Are you part of that Windsor crowd?" From the way he spoke the term it was evident that Tom didn't have much use for anyone who was.

Sandy searched for an answer. Even though "the Windsor crowd" looked down their noses at Sandy and his non-field trialing friends, geographical association said that he was guilty as accused. "Naw," he answered. "We don't have much to do with those chowderheads. We're the Fox Pass Sportsmen's Association."

"Well," Tom smiled, and clapped Sandy on the shoulder. "Glad to have you boys with us today."

They were sitting with their dogs in the morning sunshine on the clubhouse porch when Brownie's car pulled into the parking lot. It was a new '51 Ford convertible that had somehow survived the trip down the muddy road with its whitewall tires and shine intact. Walt Christian's car pulled up next to the Chevy, and next to that was Bobby Bowman's truck, with dog boxes on the back.

"Nice car," Jimmy observed.

Sandy looked from his old stove-bolt six to the new Ford, dazzling with chrome. He grinned. "I prefer running boards, myself."

"I think you left yours in that pothole back there," Jimmy replied seriously.

With little more than an exchange of nods, Brownie and his two friends walked past and into the clubhouse to sign up. As with actors, their dignity seemed controlled by a vague idea of their own importance. The door closed behind them.

"When people ask me about Mister Homer Brown," John said, "I tell them we have a nodding acquaintance—I say 'hello,' and he says 'nodding.' Me, I've stopped saying 'hello,' but I notice he still says 'nodding.' "

Minutes later, Tom Lamica opened the door of the clubhouse. "Okay—it's ten o'clock. We've got seventeen entries. If you Fox Pass fellows want to come inside, we'll have the draw."

They looked at each other for a long moment. "Fox pass?"

"I think that's what he called us—'You fox pass fellows.' "

Sandy held up his hand. "For today, we're the Fox Pass Sportsmen's Association."

They turned on Sandy. "Are you serious?"

"It was either that or be part of 'that Windsor crowd.' "

There was a silence, then Jimmy nodded. "Fine. I'll even be the president."

They started into the clubhouse. "How do you spell that—Fox Pass or faux pas?" George had a way of laughing as he spoke.

John added, "I'm not sure I even want to be a part of any association that would have a lowlife like *me* as a member."

Inside, file cards with the names of the entrants and their dogs were placed in an empty number-ten can, then drawn two at a time to determine bracemates and the order in which they would run. The two men with springers were purposely placed in the same heat, but the rest of the draw was random. When eight pairs of cards were thumbtacked to the wall, there was one card left in the can. Tom took it out and double-checked to make sure it was the last one before reading the name of the handler who would run the final heat alone. The name on the card was Sandy's.

Jimmy ran his springer, Max, in the first brace, and although Max performed in his normal workmanlike manner, the dog he was paired with ran out of control and, after wildly flushing both of the planted pheasants, chased one of them back to the pens. The rooster landed on the roof netting, and the other springer stood barking up at the bird. Jimmy just smiled and heeled Max in, but there was little humor in his eyes when he rejoined his friends on the clubhouse steps.

John had drawn the third heat against one of Brownie's dogs. Sandy went with him to the breakaway, then stood talking with Tom and the other judge while they waited for Brownie to bring his dog to the line.

"So you do this once a month. I can see where it can be fun: hunting, with a little competition thrown in."

"Competition does funny things to people." Tom lit a Lucky as he spoke. "Hunting isn't enough for 'em. To have a good time, they've got to outdo somebody at something, so they take up skeet shooting or field trialing. This . . . ," he motioned to the course they were about to run, ". . . is supposed to be just for fun, but there's some that get mighty serious about it." He lowered his voice. "Watch out for this Windsor crowd. They'll beat you to the bird field and shoot both birds if you give 'em half a chance."

"I've run with this guy before," John motioned to Brownie, who was just approaching. "I won't let him get in front of me."

❧ ☙

The back course was fairly short, and within ten minutes of breaking away John's all-white setter appeared in the bird field, with Brownie's not far behind. By the time the judges and handlers showed up, both dogs were on separate points. Brownie hurried to his setter but missed an easy shot on the pheasant. The bird sailed over the trees beyond the bird field and, in answer to the hopes of everyone who had yet to run, headed for the back course. Brownie directed his setter to where John's stood on point, hoping to get credit for a back, but John knew the game, too, and flushed his bird quickly. The shot was an easy one, and John's setter was credited with a retrieve.

❧ ☙

In the back seat of George's Chrysler, Sandy opened his thermos and poured coffee into four paper cups. "I'd say they've got you in first, John."

"Aw, it really doesn't matter much to me. I got a nice

point and saw a pretty retrieve, and for a moment I thought it was October again." He turned to Jimmy. "You and Max got a raw deal."

Jimmy waved his hand in dismissal. "You pay your two bucks and take your chances. That's the luck of the draw."

"Yeah, but it's not right." John shook his head as he handed a paper cup into the front seat. "Everybody's here to have a good time, but that guy had no business entering a dog that isn't interested in hunting."

"Well, Max hunts for my pleasure, not to impress some judge." Jimmy sipped his coffee, then added, "But still, I'd have liked a chance to make *my own* screwup."

George laughed. "You got plenty of practice last fall." The two hunted together each weekend during the hunting season. "Where is Max, by the way?"

"He's in the trunk."

Sandy grimaced. "You're as bad as George. You could have put him in my car."

Jimmy looked out the side window at Sandy's dilapidated '37 Chevy. "I offered Max that choice," he said earnestly. "But he said he'd rather the trunk."

From the car they watched as the fourth brace arrived in the bird field: Out beyond the tree line, Walt Christian's big pointer topped a rise and streaked through the bird field and out the other side without slowing down at all. He ran past the pheasant pens, circled behind the clubhouse and parking lot, and was just coming back into sight when the judges and handlers showed up. Walt was making obscure hand signals in the air, hoping to fool the judges into thinking his dog was doing just as he wanted him to. The pointer found a bird but never stopped, and although there was a moment when it appeared that the dog was going to fly into the air and catch the pheasant, at the last instant the pointer rediscovered gravity, and the bird sailed over the trees.

"You're still in first, John." Sandy had rolled down the back window and was peering out at the action. "But wait a minute . . ."

The other man's dog had pointed, then began to creep forward. The rooster could be seen walking away in the short grass. The man quickly raised his gun and strafed the pheasant, then raced his dog to the bird.

". . . No, you're safe," Sandy said.

"That guy must go through a lot of dogs." George imitated the man's shooting form. " 'Move your tail, Sparky—*ka-blam*!' "

"Yeah, he's mean all right." Sandy observed. "He probably keeps that dog in the trunk."

The day wore on, with pheasants being planted in the field in front of the clubhouse for each successive brace of dogs. And as Tom Lamica had predicted, several men who had been unlucky enough to find themselves paired with one of "the Windsor crowd" found that when they reached the bird field both of the planted pheasants had already been efficiently removed. There could be no argument that the field trailers had good dogs: With the exception of Walt Christian's flying pointer, all of them had at least one find, and Bob Bowman's classy setter had pointed three pheasants. It was the fierce competitiveness of Brownie and his friends that seemed so out of place among the casual hunters who had come to enjoy a warm winter's afternoon.

George's turn came up. After the judges had entered his name and that of his setter, George asked, "Any wild birds here?"

"There's always a few that escape from the pens. The place is pretty well hunted out during the fall, though." Tom turned to the other judge, "Sonny saw a rooster down by the swamp, when, Sonny? Last week?"

"Yeah, he was a *big* sommabitch." Sonny held his arm out to indicate that the pheasant was five feet long.

If one expects to win a field trial, one should refrain from laughing at the judges. George did not expect to win. "Jimmy," he said, "Do you have an extra deer slug? Just in case we run into this bird?"

Everyone laughed, but Sonny just looked away.

George's Llewellin was paired with a dog that appeared to be his twin. The other setter's name was Freckles, and it seemed his owner had a running argument with him as they walked the back course: "Freckles! What're you doin'? Get over here! Now get out front! What'd I tell you?! Freckles!"

George said later, "If I had a dog that was smart enough to understand all that, I wouldn't even have to take him hunting. I'd just leave a note by his doghouse and tell him what I wanted."

Freckles pointed a planted pheasant, but when his owner missed, the man took out his frustrations on the setter: the dog was put on a short lead and hauled off before the judge signaled "Pick him up."

"The poor dog." Jimmy shook his head. "I wonder what he did to deserve an owner like that."

"Maybe he was a Nazi in his last incarnation," John offered.

The last brace finished at 2:30, and after taking a five-minute breather on the porch steps, the judges got to their feet. Tom waved to Sandy. "Okay, let's have a look at that pointin' spaniel."

Sandy's friends gathered around him as he started for the breakaway. Jimmy put his hand on Sandy's shoulder. "Now listen, you've got to find more than just one bird. They must have that twerp Bowman in first with his three finds."

"Yeah, it's down to you, Sandy." John had his other shoulder. "Judges don't like to see a bye win, so you've got to do something really spectacular—find a couple birds on the back course."

Sandy smiled. "Hey, aren't you the one who said, 'Who cares about winning? We're here just to have a good time.'?"

"Yeah, but this is the Windsor crowd against . . . Who are we again? Fox Pass is it?"

Jimmy knelt on one knee as he spoke to Sandy's Brittany. "I counted five birds that flew onto the back course. Think you can find one or two, Annie?" The Brit smiled her open-mouthed dog's smile back at Jimmy, and he turned and announced, "She says, 'It's a piece of cake.' "

"How are you fixed for shells?"

Sandy dug into his jacket pocket and brought out just a pair of green paper cases.

"Two!" George took a double handful of 16-gauge shells from his own coat and put them in Sandy's pocket. "Here. These aren't doing me any good now. But remember what my grandfather used to say: 'Donna you miss the fezz.' "

Sandy worked the action of his old 97, chambering a shell. He grinned at John. "You told me this was going to be fun."

"It would be a lot of fun to beat Brownie's crowd," John said wistfully. "Find a few birds first, *then* have fun."

George waved a finger in Sandy's face as he started off: "And donna miss!"

At the breakaway Sonny looked at the Brittany and asked, "Without a tail, how do you know if she's pointing?"

Tom answered before Sandy could. "You won't have any problem. These Brittanys are supposed to be the coming thing. I remember reading something about them. They used to be poachers' dogs in France." After a moment he added, "And if that ain't the definition of a meat dog, I don't know what is."

When she was waved ahead, Annie cast to the left, into the woods, instead of straight ahead. Sandy whistled for her. When she didn't return, he left the path and went into the brush himself. Tom went with him.

The Brit was standing on a set of pheasant tracks in the snow, pointing into a barberry thicket. The pheasant got up before Sandy was in position, and—unsure of where the judge was—he hesitated until he heard Tom behind him saying, "Shoot, dammit!" The bird tumbled at the sound of his gun, and Annie brought it in.

They came out of the woods into an open field that was the back course. The weight of the pheasant in Sandy's game pocket did little to ease the tension he felt. He knew he was supposed to be enjoying this, but he felt not only the scrutiny of the judges but also the critical eyes of the several watchers who trailed along behind in entourage fashion. In the snow the footprints of the other hunters who had passed earlier showed they all had followed an old cart road along the wooded edge. Sandy tried to picture where a pheasant that had been flushed and missed in the bird field would have flown. He whistled to his dog and angled across the field, making new tracks in the snow as he went.

The Brit crossed a low stone fence and cast ahead on the far side. Suddenly she turned and pointed back at the wall. A pheasant ran out from between the rocks, saw the men, and sprung into the air. Sandy waited. Then, when the bird was at the top of its climb, he centered the rooster. Annie was there when the pheasant hit the ground and brought it proudly to her handler.

"I'll carry that for you—you don't want to get weighted down." Tom winked as he spoke. He turned to Sonny, "Any questions about how a Brittany points without benefit of a tail?"

"No." The other judge shook his head. "But shouldn't the dog wait to be told to retrieve?"

Tom laughed. "Sure. But this, Sonny, is a real meat dog." He motioned to Sandy. "Go ahead up to the bird field."

Minutes later, as they were crossing back toward the cart road, the Brit caught scent and began working toward a cattail swamp below the field. Sandy turned to Tom. "She's got a runner. I'd like to follow her."

"I'll kick you in the pants if you don't."

Just a few scattered patches of snow remained in this end of the field, but here and there the tracks of a pheasant were intermingled with the Brittany's. The field ended abruptly at a beaver pond, with the swamp stretching away beyond. The dog stopped, pointing into a seemingly barren patch of snow.

"She's got him pinned." Having said it, Sandy now tried to believe it himself. Tentatively, he approached the point. The rooster that had somehow hidden himself in the sparse grass jumped into the afternoon sky. The shot was an easy one, but the bird took a pair of hits before falling, just as Sandy was about to fire for the third time.

The pheasant lay across the pond in plain sight, but Annie veered into the cattails when she was sent after it. When Sandy whistled and waved her to the left, she paused only long enough to glance back at him. He recognized the signs and quickly searched his pockets for more of George's shells.

His Brit could be heard breaking through thin ice in the swamp, then there was a pause and yet another pheasant clattered into the air in an extravaganza of color and noise. Sonny had exaggerated the size of the rooster but not by much: The bird had in-curved spurs and a half-inch of fringe on his yard-long tail feathers. Later, however, the part Sandy remembered most clearly was the way the bird's wings struck the head of a cattail as it sprung from the frozen swamp, causing a small cloud of fluff to float on the breeze afterward. That, and the unforgettable image of Annie coming out of the weeds into the December sunshine with the copper-breasted bird held high.

As Sandy entered the bird field with the judges close behind him, carrying the four pheasants, the scene could have been out of a Rudyard Kipling story. Annie hunted through the maze of old scent in the field to find the one pheasant that had been planted just for her. Sandy lifted his cap and approached her point. His phantoms of tension had vanished, and he grinned as he recalled John's parting words: He was now going to have some fun.

The pheasant flushed and crossed the field, gaining the altitude it needed to clear the tall maples beyond. The moment passed when he ordinarily would have taken the bird, and the cross shot became a quartering shot that had turned into a very long, going-away shot when Sandy finally put the 97 to his shoulder and fired. There was an instant when he was sure he'd missed, and he regretted showing off on this last bird . . . but then the shot string caught the pheasant and it fell through the bare branches, tumbling to finally land beyond the wall at the edge of the field.

George and Jimmy and John came out into the bird field to shake Sandy's hand. Amid the laughter, brags, and praise Annie delivered the final pheasant of the day to her master. After Sandy took the bird from her, he lifted his dog in his arms. "You're a good girl, Annie."

"I guess she is!" John scratched the Brit's ears.

"Look at that." Jimmy pointed to the parking lot, where the three vehicles of the Windsor crowd were just pulling out.

George laughed. "I guess they're not going to stick around to find out who took second and third."

Sandy put his dog back on the ground, and they all started toward the clubhouse. "So what do you think of this pointin' spaniel, judge?"

"My hat's off to her," said Sonny. "Tom's right—she's a real meat dog."

"Meat dog, hell," Tom said. "That is one mighty fine *bird* dog."

DAVID KENNEY first hunted quail in the 1930s, in southern Illinois, and was fortunate to marry into a quail-hunting family. He and his wife, Wanda, have owned pointing dogs since 1952, and there have been one or more Brittanys in their household continuously since 1962.

For much of his career, David has earned a living teaching political science at Southern Illinois University, but for eight years (1977–84) he was the director of the Illinois Department of Conservation.

The Kenneys' current Brittany is a six year old named Rob, a-sixth generation descendent of their first. David and Wanda recently broke with tradition and went outside their line to acquire a new pup, Billy.

"Memories Are Made of Things Like These" was originally published in the *American Brittany* magazine, April 1999.

Memories Are Made of Things Like These

by David Kenney

Increasingly stiff and creaky knees led me and Cousin Bill to purchase a John Deere "Gator," a four-wheeled all-terrain vehicle with a windshield, bucket seats for two, and ample space behind for two dog boxes, set side by side. There is even room enough between each box and the side panel of the bed to slide a gun case. The wide, deep, open glove compartment makes a fine bird box. Altogether, this vehicle is a great convenience for two aging hunters.

That year, "the quail law," as the old-timers used to call opening day, came on Saturday, November 7. The day was a perfect one—clear and brisk and dry, with a sky blue enough to dazzle the eye and cheer the heart. Neal and I went into the Beaucoup creek bottom with the Gator to shoot some liberated quail.

We found a long strip of grassy cover bordering a large soybean field where the harvester had already done its work. Notably, several rows of bean stalks had been left standing here and there for the bobwhite to feed on. That's the kind of consideration that young men who are also bird hunters will often indulge in as they harvest their crops.

The grassy strip, ranging from ten to twenty yards in

width, was permanent cover. It was left alone because of a USDA subsidy program that was intended to improve stream quality through the reduction of erosion and chemical runoff. This particular cover strip separated the bean field from a narrow band of trees that ran along the creek and varied in width as the water course swung one way, then the other.

The patch of cover was about three-eighths of a mile long, and in many places the weeds stood waist high. We put two wire bird boxes—each containing ten quail—on the tailgate of the Gator. Two hundred yards along the field edge we stopped. Neal placed one of the cages on the ground at the edge of the cover, swung its wire gate open, and tapped the back. We watched as five birds scuttled out into the weeds, disappearing from sight almost immediately.

We repeated that procedure twice, the second time near the very end of the cover strip. Then back along the field edge we went, making good speed over the almost bare bean ground. We dropped the last five birds in a brushy corner of woods located an eighth of a mile in the opposite direction from our truck, where the dogs were impatiently waiting to be released. In all, we distributed twenty quail in groups of five over a distance of about half a mile.

We returned to the vehicle, slipped our guns out of their cases, pocketed shells, and opened the dog-box doors. Rob and Bell hit the ground running.

We hunted the birds in the order they had been put down. This is always good procedure since they may decide to move a substantial distance from the release point. Or they may be scattered or even decimated by a passing hawk or coyote.

Just as dogs experienced in finding quail should, the

two Brittanys set to work industriously, running the edges of the weed strip and those of the thicket that marked its inner border. Rob and Bell were into the first groups of birds within five minutes.

The hunt went on routinely but had its share of exciting moments, as one dog then the other went on point, its bracemate honoring the find. At least twice we had both Rob and Bell pointing at once—not far apart but each on a separate bird. At such times, we divided our attention between the two dogs and were gratified to see each one in turn stand fast while its bracemate's bird was flushed and killed.

At the easternmost bend of the creek we got into the last group of five quail that we had put down. Three rose at one time. Two fell to the guns, but the third—untouched—made a short flight into the fringe of trees bordering the water. Neal took Bell toward it, and in a moment, her search was successful.

At the flush, the quail swung out over the creek. Neal's gun came up, and the bird fell just at the top of the steep embankment on the other side. It hit the ground hard, then rolled down the slope and into the water.

With the trees still half in leaf, Bell had not seen the bird fly or fall. Neal surveyed the scene for a moment, then heeled his dog fifty yards downstream, where a large sandbar went halfway across. He sent her into the few yards of water that separated him from the other side.

Bell went readily, wading at first then swimming, encouraged by Neal's throwing motions and his calls of "Fetch, fetch!" When the dog reached the other side of the creek, Neal directed her with arm signals up the bank, then along level ground toward where the bird had fallen.

The Brittany scented the quail while she was still on top of the bank. When Neal called out, "Dead bird, dead bird!" Bell went directly down the bank and stepped into the water. After swimming a stroke or two, she mouthed the dead quail and turned back toward dry land. Then the dog went back up the bank, turned along its top, came back to the narrows where she had crossed, and completed her retrieve to our side of the stream.

By that time, Neal and I were standing in the fringe of trees on the top of the bank. Bell came directly toward us and laid the bird in Neal's hand. It had been a splendid exhibition of canine sagacity.

We stood there in the morning sunshine of that early November day for a moment or two, savoring the little drama we had just witnessed. We were almost a mile from the nearest dwelling. It was profoundly quiet there in the Beaucoup bottom, with its fields of bean and corn stubble, its woodlots, and the wooded strips along its sloughs and the creek itself. Great sycamore trees shone white-trunked in the sunlight. The sky overhead was as blue as it ever gets.

"Memories," said Neal, "are made of things like these."

TRED SLOUGH is a pen name for and figment of the imagination of one Robert Holthouser of Surry County, North Carolina. In his mind's eye, Tred is a handsome, sharp-eyed man who keeps himself in top physical condition. He is a crack shotgunner and a natural dog trainer. Game birds from ruffed grouse to ringneck pheasants tremble when Tred enters the woods or fields with one of his marvelously biddable Brittanys.

Robert, on the other hand, describes himself as a middle-aged, native Carolinian with poor eyesight and rapidly thinning hair. Grouse sometimes giggle at his approach. A carpenter by trade, Robert has been accused of wasting much of his adult life simply wandering the country, fishing, and bird hunting in order that he might sit beside a campfire at night drinking beer and talking to his dogs. He confesses to that charge but defends himself by saying that he does not consider any of those activities to be a waste.

Tred Slough stories have appeared in *Gray's Sporting Journal, Shooting Sportsman,* and *Sporting Classics.* Robert, Tred, and Down East Books are currently collaborating on a book to be titled *A High Lonesome Sound.*

The stories "Road Hunter" and "Groucho" are original, previously unpublished pieces.

Road Hunter

by Tred Slough

Take it easy, boy." Kenneth Parker put a hand on the trembling shoulder of his best friend. The Brittany was trying to stand on the seat as the pickup rippled along the washboard road, but he was not strong enough to maintain that precarious posture for long. When his hindquarters buckled under the strain he would sit for a while on his haunches and prop himself upright with stiff front legs. Each time the truck began to straighten after exiting a curve the dog would rise and brace himself by pressing his silver muzzle against the dashboard. His cloudy eyes then searched the shoulders of the road until another curve or bump crumpled him, forcing him to rest until his heart commanded that he stand once more and search for whatever lay around the next bend.

Parker knew that the Brittany's eyesight was almost gone; he also knew that there is more than one kind of vision. As the man and the dog fled the rooster tail of dust that followed them, they looked through the dirty windshield and saw all the years they had traveled together.

At a turnout where an old logging trail joined the haul road, Parker stopped. The dog waited for the passenger door to open before he climbed stiffly to the floorboard and felt his way to the ground. From a kennel crate in the back of the truck a young dog, one of the old one's many sons, complained loudly as the man snapped his double gun together and followed the old-timer down the muddy track.

They moved very slowly—the dog thirty yards ahead of the man—for fifteen minutes before Parker whistled to his partner, calling him in. On the way back to the truck the dog walked alongside the hunter, who spoke to him in a low voice.

"Whatta ya' think old man? You a pretty good boy? Think I ought to leave that kid in the truck don't you? Let you kill yourself in that swamp eh?" They walked together silently for a few minutes before the man spoke again. "Can't do it, old-timer; I just can't do it, Pete."

The dog wagged his stubby tail briefly at each word he recognized: "Old man," "Good boy," and his name. At the truck he lay down hard on his side and begged silently to not go in the crate. When the tailgate opened and the youngster bounded out, he did not move. Parker picked up the old dog and put him in the kennel.

The young dog was fast and beautiful. His coat glistened amid the damp ferns as he swept back and forth, hunting both sides of the trail. Parker let him work off some of his great energy until they reached the spot where he had made the old dog turn back. Then he called Jake in.

The little dog strained against the man's hands as Parker attached a small bell to his collar. Taut muscles under the thick fur quivered as the hunter stroked the dog's flanks, trying to harness the youthful excitement. "Okay Jake. Hunt close now. Find us a bird." The little dog was off the instant he was released.

Ankle-deep water covered the trail where it crossed a meadow that had been taken over by tag alder. The ruts from past logging operations were deeper still, and the hunter picked his way slowly while the dog got farther and farther ahead. Where the land began to rise, a few aspen and spruce climbed above the shrubs. Parker heard two grouse flush well in front of him. A flash of orange and white appeared and stopped in the trail. The dog looked first in the direction the birds had flown, then back to Parker.

The hunter walked by the dog without speaking. Years ago when he was first training the old one he had often lost his temper over the kind of poor work the youngster had just displayed. The man knew now that anger and loud words were counterproductive. He also knew how lucky he was that Pete had been stubborn enough to learn in spite of having such a poor teacher. This last son was much softer, his psyche almost delicate, and Parker walked well beyond the dog before he whistled him up to hunt again.

The trail wound along the edge of a low hill dotted with paper birch that gleamed white and leafless. On the man's left, the dog worked a swampy cut-over where more alders crowded young aspens and sheltered the tender greens that fed the grouse. Parker gave in to the rhythms of walking and remembering. His mind wandered other trails, moving back to the days when Old Pete was in his prime. The tinkle of the young dog's bell was steady and constant, a flowing sound that became unheard until it stopped.

Sudden silence brought the hunter back from his reverie. He looked for the dog where he last remembered hearing the bell and found him a few yards off the trail. "Good boy, Jake. Whoa-up."

The man gave the unnecessary command in a soft, re-assuring tone as he stepped past the pointing dog. The flush seemed to occur in slow motion as the bird struggled through the thick growth. Parker tracked the sound with his gun barrels and fired just as the grouse cleared the tops of the spalling aspens. An easy shot.

As he watched Jake make the retrieve, Parker tried to not compare him to his sire. He failed, as he had many times before. The young dog was better looking, had a bet-ter nose, and hunted with a graceful, high-headed style. But something was missing—a spark, a fire, something that had made Parker fall in love with the old dog and pre-vented him from doing so with this one. He reminded him-self that Jake was young, that there was still a chance he might someday show the heart that was old Pete's greatest asset. Someday. Maybe. Even without that heart he was still a better bird dog. Parker didn't really care. He didn't want a better dog. He wanted old Pete to be young again.

The trail skirted the swamp for another half-mile before it rose to circle the birches and the spruce. The damp earth held scent well, and another grouse fell to the dog and the gun.

When they reached the higher ground, Parker sat down to rest. The young dog was not ready to stop; he did not come in to lay his head across the man's knee but waited impatiently fifteen yards away, his attention fo-cused ahead. Parker closed his eyes and looked back, to a campfire in Ontario, a marsh in Alaska, a dry creek bed where he and Pete had hunkered down out of a wind that swept the high northern plains. In his mind he traced the years and miles back to the dark, sweet-smelling Appalachian hollows where he first followed a hardheaded puppy that taught him how to hunt.

When he opened his eyes he saw Jake farther down the trail, standing on point. Parker went to the dog and stepped past him with his gun at port arms. The grouse flushed from a thicket of ferns behind them. The man spun to get off a quick shot. At first the bird did not appear to be hit, then it turned straight up, flying vertically until it became a silver silhouette against the sky. High above the man and the dog the ascent stopped, yet still the wings fought on. For frozen seconds the bird hung in the air, straining, like Icarus, toward an impossible zenith. The solid black band on the fanned tail showed sharp and clear in a shaft of sunshine that cut the clouds like a searchlight. Suspended, the grouse resisted the pull of the earth, dead and alive at the same time. Parker watched as the wings briefly beat faster still, then faltered. The hole in the cloudbank closed as the life slipped away. When the bird hit the ground it was only dead.

He worked the young dog for two more hours. Purposefully he pushed away from the damp covers toward harder ground. He did not want to kill another grouse that day; he wanted only to tire Jake so that he would give no trouble in camp.

The dog worked well for a while before losing interest in the dry, scentless woods. Finally he gave up completely and came in to walk at the man's heels. Parker spoke to him in a pleasant voice, but his words were not kind. "You're a quitter, you know that Jake. Things get a little tough and you just give up." The dog wagged his tail at the man's tone of voice and at the sound of his name. He followed closely on the long walk back to the road. When they passed through the swamp where they had such success earlier, Jake picked up faint scents drifting across the trail, but he did not stray from the man's tracks to hunt again. He was tired.

When they reached the truck, Jake jumped immediately in the back and waited for Parker to open the kennel. Father and son sniffed each other briefly as Pete came out and Jake went in. The old dog walked stiffly to the tailgate and sniffed the man's vest. Parker showed him the birds one by one.

"Your boy did pretty good old man. Bumped a couple, but we know all about that don't we? He's gonna be all right I guess. Just needs a little drive. Know what I mean?"

Pete wagged his tail to the patter, his milky eyes fixed on Parker, until the man picked him up and put him on the ground. Stumbling a little, the dog found a clump of moss that he marked without raising his leg, then started into the woods. Thirty yards away he sat down and looked back to the truck. The hunter put the dead grouse in the cooler before putting his vest back on. Clicking his gun closed, he followed Pete down the trail. Again they walked for only fifteen minutes, long enough for the dog to empty his bowels and to imagine that he could still hunt.

When they returned, Parker helped the dog onto the seat. He drove slowly toward his camp, thinking about the bird that had "towered" earlier that day—how it had struggled to fly on even though it was dead, how the break in the clouds had illuminated the last wingbeats so beautifully. Unconsciously Parker stroked old Pete's trembling flanks as he drove. Bracing himself by pressing his silver muzzle hard against the dashboard, the dog once more searched the shadows along the edge of the road.

Groucho

by Tred Slough

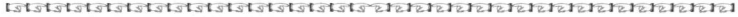

The last thing I needed was another dog. When it became obvious that I was going to get stuck with Groucho, I made up my mind that even though I would end up training him and treating him well, I wasn't going to like him very much.

Groucho is a Brittany, out of decent parents but from an unplanned family, the result of doors and gates poorly latched. He earned his name early. While the other pups mewed and squeaked, this one grumbled and clawed his way to his mother's teats. He competed well enough to grow along with his siblings, but he had been born with an affliction called entropion, which caused his lower eyelids to constantly push against his eyeballs, making it appear that his eyes never fully opened. When his brothers and sisters moved on to new homes, Groucho was unwanted at any price.

A trip to the vet corrected his problem and then some. The good doctor cut and pulled and stitched the skin below his eyes until the lower lids drooped, purposely over-correcting in the hope that the proper balance might be attained as the puppy matured. Concern that the offending condition might return proved unfounded, and the dog has gone through life with a bad attitude about veterinarians and a face that looks as if he is always coming off a three-day drunk. Once I got used to it, I began to sort of enjoy Groucho's hungover appearance. Every time I look at him I am reminded of certain people I know who suffer through similar conditions with a wry smile of recognition that they got their headaches from too much fun, even as they vow to never do it again.

Although he is a happy enough little fellow now, the pup's initial reaction to a world that greeted him with a poke in the eye was to growl at it. It was the only sound he knew how to make, and he used it for all occasions. He was particularly vocal around a friend of mine who had the misfortune of being the first person Groucho saw when the anesthesia from his surgery was wearing off. The dog eventually figured out that my friend is not the man who cut his face into a goofy caricature of a hound, and they are big buddies now. Still, when Wally comes around and is greeted by a wagging tail, Groucho still remembers to growl just a little bit, too.

A contrarian nature and bumbling expression were Groucho's most redeeming characteristics for a long time. He went through his childhood lessons well enough and showed plenty of nose, but he was not a hard worker. The pup was more dilettantish than diligent and drifted through adolescence with a disturbing tendency to stay out late at night and shirk his responsibilities in the field.

Every dog needs a job, however, and Groucho eventually found his niche as the redheaded stepchild of my hunting family. He became a backup player to Stranger, another Brittany, an old-timer who hunts with a desire and heart that mask his barely average ability. When the favored one would climb into the front seat of the truck two days in a row, young Groucho went cheerfully to his kennel, either confident that the third day would be his or, more likely, not smart enough to realize that I was going hunting without him.

As time went on, the expeditions that satisfied my addiction to the smell of burnt powder became longer and more widespread. The sweet little darlin' at home made it clear that my absence would nurture a lot more fondness if I took both dogs with me, so Groucho was added to the traveling retinue.

For several years the dog box in the back of the truck was his vacation home. He accepted it with the same resigned willingness he showed toward his kennel when the old man traveled in the front seat and got most of the work. Groucho rode the bench for five years without showing a sign of wanting to be on the first team. He got just enough work to stay in shape and went contentedly back to the sidelines as soon as Stranger had rested enough to return to the game.

This year the old dog has begun to show his age for the first time. I knew it was coming—the silver around the muzzle, the stiffness on the stairs. It's going to be hard on me, but time cannot be stopped or even slowed. Although I tried in the beginning of Stranger's life not to like him either, that attempt failed long ago. He won my respect with his effort and eventually won my heart with his chin across my knee and my hand on the back of his neck as we shared travels and campfires and silent recollections of the sound of wings. Stranger's getting old is bad enough, but now Groucho has figured it out, too.

The first sign that he might want to be even slightly better than ordinary came late last year. We were working an overgrown logging road when I came around the corner to find Groucho stopped—not actually pointing but refusing to go ahead. As I stepped past him, a grouse came off the hillside far in front, and I stretched the right barrel enough to knock it down. I could hear the bird running in the leaves, and although Groucho took off in pursuit, he had always been a haphazard retriever. I was kicking myself for taking such a long shot and not making a clean kill. The sound of the dog's bell faded and disappeared for several minutes before it began to grow louder again. The little dummy made the long climb up the slope and dropped the bird at my feet. The shower of praise he received failed to cleanse him of his multitudinous sins however, and he returned to mediocrity for the rest of the day—and the remainder of the season, as well.

This October, with the leaves on the Blue Ridge Mountains refusing to fall at my command, we headed north to Wisconsin. The old dog tired after only a half day in the flat country and did not argue when I helped him into the truck to swap places with his son. The afternoon belonged to Groucho. With the first-stringer out and the game still in question, he rose to the occasion. Ignoring the lure of two birds that flushed wild as we worked our way through a thick swamp, he carefully hunted the edges of the muddy trails that wound through old clearcuts. Three times he found grouse, nailing them solidly, and each time the bird cleared the tops of the tag alders, the shot was true and the retrieve made with confidence. We quit early, with daylight remaining and good cover ahead, because I did not want to push the string of luck the dog and I were both enjoying.

Back at the pickup, I let the tailgate down and put the

birds in the cooler. When I opened the door to put my gun behind the seat, Groucho leaped in. Since it was only a little way back to camp I decided to humor him and let him ride in the front seat instead of inside the box in the back, where he knew he belonged.

We roamed Wisconsin and then North Dakota for a few more weeks, and Groucho continued to perform fairly well. He still showed a tendency to false point and to hesitate too long over old scent, and his retrieves usually involved a couple of stops along the way back. But there was no doubt that that he had gotten better. His share of the workload increased too, but Stranger hunted his way back into shape, and our long-standing partnership was once more secure. When the snow began to fall in the Dakotas and we turned southeast toward the Appalachians, the old dog was still getting the first chance afield and the favored spot on the passenger side of the seat.

Like the walnut tree in my yard, the hickories and locusts had shed their leaves by the time we returned to the foothills of the Blue Ridge. The oaks and maples were losing ground, as well, and tormented me with colorful showers as I went about the overdue tasks involved in preparing for the winter. The trees were bare at the higher elevations, and the young grouse had left their summer haunts to look for berries, frosted grapes, and tender greens. At last the lady of the house deemed the storerooms and the woodpile sufficient, and the dogs and I fled to the hills.

Stranger hunted the steep covers as hard as ever, but at the end of the day he was stumbling where once he ran and was searching for ways around fallen trees he had leaped over just last year. We found birds though—three of them fell before the gun and the dog that first afternoon back in the mountains. Then, on the second day, when I put the old one up at noon he did not complain.

Groucho missed his first chance, but I didn't blame him for it. The grouse came out of a tree twenty feet over my head and I missed, emptying both barrels at close range in thick cover and then counting the feathers on the bird's tail as it slipped through an opening thirty yards away. Groucho responded to the sound of the gun and began to hunt hard, showing an enthusiasm not always present in years past. Ten minutes later the bell on his collar fell silent a hundred yards in front of me. When I reached the saddle in the ridgeline where he stood, I found Groucho not pointed but standing in his old "I think there's something here but I'm not sure where" posture.

I walked past and below him before stopping to wait for the flush. None came and when I whistled him on, Groucho ran down the hill. He was searching the area where I suspected the birds to be when grouse began to flush from the hillside we had just left. Six birds took off—one at a time and twenty yards out of range. With great effort I managed to keep my tone of voice level as I called Groucho in and told him I would be most appreciative if he would give me better directions than, "They're around here somewhere, boss."

I was not surprised that he failed to get the message, and when a few minutes later he stopped again with his tail wagging and looked at me over his shoulder, I stepped up beside him to give him his job description one more time. "Groucho, you are an idiot. If you're going to wait for me to come along and tell you which bush they're under, you might as well carry the damn gun and strap the bell around *my* neck."

I was telling him off pretty good when the reasons for the dog's hesitancy began to erupt. We were surrounded, and four grouse flushed in concert—one right, one left, and two straight ahead. I recovered in time to get one of the straight-aways, and Groucho went directly to the downed bird and brought it to me.

This unexpected success didn't diminish my opinion that the little dog was never going to be a big-time player, that he was too afraid of making a mistake to hunt with the verve that makes the good ones so special. It never occurred to me that the scent he had detected earlier might have come from one of the birds just flushed, or that he had made the right decision by just stopping when there were lots of birds around us but very little cover that might convince them to hold.

We crossed the ridge and spent another hour looking for the first bunch of grouse that had scattered behind us. Groucho worked well and managed a point on the two that we found, but they were jumpy and I was not able to get close enough for a shot. With the afternoon waning we worked our way back to the hillside above the truck, where the dog began to hesitate again. I told him to go ahead, and fifteen yards later he slammed into a picture-perfect stance. I knew when I pulled the trigger that I was a shade slow. The bird tumbled, but the feathers hanging in the air came mostly from the grouse's tail. Groucho was fumbling in the bushes where the bird fell when I heard it take off again.

The Brittany ran in circles for a while, but I gave him no encouragement. Too many times in the past I had seen him start a retrieve only to put the bird down and roll on his back in self-indulgence. Although Groucho was out of sight when he first went for the retrieve, I knew it had happened again, and this time it cost us a bird—a grouse with no tail feathers and two broken legs, one that would feed a fox family before sunrise the next day.

I didn't say anything, just started back to the truck with the little dummy moping along behind. As I was taking off my vest I looked back to make sure he was following and saw him standing in the middle of the trail I had just walked down. His goofy face and the fresh memory of the lost bird did not make me happy. I put the first grouse in the cooler and opened the truck door before turning back to the dog. "Are you coming or not?" I didn't say it in a particularly pleasant tone of voice. Groucho picked up a dead grouse with no tail and two broken legs from between his feet and trotted to the back of the truck, where he put it down. As I looked at the bird in amazement, he jumped into the cab and stretched out on the seat.

On the ride home I had to scoot a little to my left to make room for both Brittanys, and my right hand alternated between soft necks. I can get used to being sort of crowded, I guess. It looks like my only choice. I can't afford a bigger truck.

CHARLEY WATERMAN is undoubtedly one of our finest outdoor writers. Born in 1913, he was raised on a farm in southeastern Kansas. After high school and college, Charley was for a short time a professional wrestler and a newspaper reporter and photographer.

Following World War II, he did some news photography in the San Francisco area and fished and hunted the Sierras. In 1952 Charley and his wife, Debie, settled in northern Florida, and he began a full-time writing career. The Watermans routinely traveled to other parts of the country in pursuit of upland birds with gun dogs. They spent considerable time in Montana, often behind Brittanys from the kennel of fellow outdoor writer Ben O. Williams.

Charley has written countless magazine articles over the past fifty years and has received the Excellence in Craft award from the Outdoor Writers Association of America. In addition, he is a regular columnist for seven outdoor magazines and is the author of eighteen books. The latest, *Gun Dogs & Bird Guns,* is a collection of stories that focus on upland hunting.

The two stories included in this anthology, "Business Associate" and "Old Kelly," originally appeared in Charley's book *The Part I Remember,* published in 1974. The story *Me and Clyde* first appeared in *Gun Dog,* October/November 1995.

Business Associate
by Charley Waterman

There is a point at which a mature and intelligent hunting dog may begin to replace his instincts with reasoning, and it is such dogs that become legends.

Perhaps there is no thrill to compare to a puppy's first point. He has stopped and stood because some intangible thing from ancestors long gone has frozen his muscles. When it first happens I wonder what goes through his puppy brain, for he is a sort of innocent observer of the whole thing—probably amazed that this scent has made him rigid when the smell of a bone only makes him hungry. To the unscientific hunter, the instincts of pointing and retrieving are unparalleled examples of heredity, and while training shapes and polishes them, they have been there all along.

But this brings us to the other things, the beginnings of which set a dog apart. There is the retriever who decides without guidance that dead birds must be brought to the particular individual who fired the shot—or perhaps he must decide the downed game should be divided equally among the hunters, no matter how much trouble it becomes. And there is the unprogrammed business of a pointing dog's jumping straight up and down to flush a nearby pheasant when the hunter is close by and the bird might otherwise run instead of flying. At that moment a pointer borrows from the flushing breeds.

Then there is the very attitude of pointing, and there are great old bird finders who do their work in very relaxed form, no longer galvanized into classic poses by the magic scent but simply reporting the presence of game because they know it is there and because the shooter wants to know.

McGillicuddy, the old Brittany, had all of these perceptive habits, the frivolous business of pointing style having lost its importance long before. The porcelain point had given way to a calm indication of where he thought the Huns or sage grouse should be. McGillicuddy would mark a plunging chukar covey until the birds were only specks in a Washington chasm, and if someone had fired and one bird had landed short of the rest he'd start the precipitous journey without urging. You could say that McGillie knew what was going on.

There was the time when I had no dog, and the mallard drake surprised me. He got up from a narrow, deep section of creek and didn't hang up there the way jumping mallards sometimes do. Instead, the duck went off low across a close-grazed stretch of grass on the other side, a nearly bare area that measured fifty yards across and was surrounded by brush and timber, except where the creek bordered a little of it.

It hadn't seemed that I was quite on with my shot, but the mallard came down near the center of the opening and lay flat in the grass without moving. I watched it for a couple of minutes, then went upstream to find a shallow crossing place. Of course when I came back to the open spot the mallard was gone, leaving only half a dozen gray feathers. It was a crippled bird, I had been stupid, and I spent almost an hour probing nearby brush, feeling sure the cripple would be hidden within a few feet of the open ground. The adjacent section of creek offered no visible concealment.

So with the self-accusation that always goes with cripples, I trudged unhappily back to my car and drove ten miles to town for McGillicuddy. Almost two hours after the duck had fallen I brought him to the half-dozen feathers and tried to explain the situation. McGillie listened attentively, his tongue sticking straight out a quarter of an inch as it always does when there is a knotty problem. He declined to sniff the feathers.

He didn't vacuum the ground as he usually does when someone mentions a dead bird. And he paid no attention to the fifty-yard clearing. Even humans could find a bird there. He trotted briskly around the perimeter, almost all the way, with his head high. Then he stopped still on the creek side, looked straight at me and made an elaborate point toward the creek; then looked at me again. Together we walked to the water's edge. I could see nothing there and the banks were close-cropped. McGillie was eyeing me instead of the water.

Then he trotted upstream to an easy entry spot and came paddling down to near where I stood, turned into the bank and almost disappeared. Only his stub tail and his energetically working hind legs showed. It was an unseen undercut and he finally managed to back out with the duck. We went back to town, McGillie napping on the back seat.

Of course he had scented the mallard—or had scented

its route to the creek, taken nearly two hours before—and figured out the rest. I put him back in the kennel with courtesy and respect. I don't own McGillicuddy but I wish I did.

But then maybe nobody really owns a personality like that. He's sort of a business associate.

Old Kelly

by Charley Waterman

I have not been noted for sentimentality, but my bifocals steamed up a little today—over a speckled dog.

He's getting old now, and he never has had the nobility of Lassie or the classic pointing stance of Gunsmoke. He's just been an honest bird dog, and although there have been a lot better, none ever tried harder and there never was a more agreeable associate.

Today he loped down a sun-baked South Dakota hill where a hot, dry wind was bending the prairie grass. In the bottom of the draw was a little brush where a game bird might find shade at midday, and down there old Kelly—a Brittany—slowed a little, wiggled his stub tail, then pointed, his tongue lolling almost to the ground.

When I walked up, some brown birds almost as large as pheasants came out with guttural cackling, and I shot one. Then, wonder of wonders, I managed to get another before they swept over a shoulder of the draw. Kelly ran over to one bird, nosed it, and lay down beside it, completely tuckered out.

It was just another kind of bird to Kelly, but it was the last on a long list I'd made up several years ago when I decided I'd try to shoot every kind of upland game bird in

North America over the same dog. Some of them hadn't come easily, like the Mearns quail Kelly pointed in Arizona when only three of his legs were working. He was so crippled up after that day in the desert that we took him to the veterinary and feared he'd never again use four legs. But, as usual, old Kelly came through and was back on the job six months later.

Then there was the time in Alaska when he went over a cliff after a hard-hit ptarmigan. And the time he rammed the stick into his eye in British Columbia (he never did watch where he was going).

Now, shooting all the species of upland birds in North America is not high adventure. Anyone could do it if he were persistent enough, and any dog could point them all if he were reasonably adaptable and someone put him in the right place. I got the idea because I was going to write some stuff about upland hunting and figured the best way to learn about it was to do it.

Now I'll give you my list. There may be some readers who won't quite agree that this is all of the birds, but except for subspecies and slight variations, this list was the best I could make. And the bird that old Kelly lay down beside today was the true prairie chicken, an appropriate bird to finish out with because it's one of the most unusual characters of the upland classification. And because it is fighting a tough battle to make a living as civilization continues to trim the grazing lands.

The list of birds goes like this:

Bobwhite quail, Mearns quail, valley quail, scaled quail, Gambel's quail, mountain quail, woodcock, sharptail grouse, ruffed grouse, blue grouse, Franklin's grouse, sage grouse, Hungarian partridge, chukar partridge, ptarmigan, pheasant, snipe, and prairie chicken. That makes eighteen. There are other upland birds that aren't often hunted with dogs. We got some of those, too.

I get tired of hearing men brag about their dogs, and I won't bore you any longer with this. I'm going to get old Kelly off my left foot, where he's taking a nap. Then I am going to put this old portable typewriter on the bed in this little South Dakota motel, and I'm going out and buy my dog a steak—well, some hamburger, anyway.

The above was written shortly before old Kelly left us forever. The hills and hedges haven't been quite the same since.

Me and Clyde

by Charley Waterman

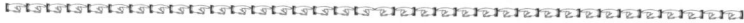

If you want a crash course in field performance and training, borrow a bird dog, but only from a good friend of long standing, one who possesses endless tolerance. It might work better if he owes you money.

This experience might not be too good for the dog, and I don't recommend it, although I recently borrowed Clyde, a personable and leggy Brittany. His owner did not owe me money. I borrowed Clyde because I was far from home with no dog of my own and had an irresistible desire to chase some Hungarian partridges. I vowed that I would not try to alter Clyde's approach to birds, and I don't think he learned much. I learned quite a bit. It was the same as starting out with a freshly purchased dog that had been handled by someone else for some time.

At the start of our day together, I took Clyde to the rear of the truck, where he faced the open door of the dog box.

"Load up!" I said.

Clyde looked puzzled.

"He's used to 'Kennel up!' " my wife explained sweetly from behind me.

Okay. From then on, I swore I would try nothing Clyde had not heard before. In fact, I decided to let him take charge of the whole project. It was a learning experience—for me, that is. Clyde proved to be a very good dog. He is not perfect, but I have hunted with no perfect dogs.

The important part is that I accepted Clyde as is and began to think about the things pointing dogs are expected to do and about how those things vary from handler to handler and from bird to bird.

Clyde's owner says he's a soft dog, and I guess he is. That doesn't mean Clyde whimpers and quivers when confused. It means simply that Clyde tolerates human frailty and does not bite when given a stupid command. He thinks I am strange but harmless, and on our hunt he appeared sympathetic when I did things the wrong way. The farther we went, the less I bothered him.

Clyde's range was about right for the open country, and when I was about to bawl him out for circling to my rear, I realized he was just checking my scent so he wouldn't lose me. Sometimes he did that when I thought he could see me plainly, but it was Clyde's show and that was part of his routine. Did he trust his nose more than his eyes, or was it just a habit of his? That's Clyde's business, and I'm not his trainer.

At first, Clyde frequently stopped and stood for several seconds, looking back where we had come from. He would do this several times, whenever we left the truck. A more observant soul than I finally explained that Clyde had always worked with other dogs and that when I took him out by himself he expected company at any moment. The third time out he evidently decided the hunt was up to him alone, and he quit expecting assistants to show up.

Clyde checked in with me frequently, and after he'd done it several times from a reasonable distance, I decided to call him in for a drink and a little rest. When I blew my whistle, he came to full attention about seventy-five yards away. But he didn't come to me, so I called him by name several times. He just stood and stared. Mutiny?

No, it wasn't mutiny at all. He was used to having his name called very sharply, with exclamation points. When I became impatient and yelled his name as if I'd lost my temper, he came in at high speed. He wasn't scared. It was just the way he had always been called. And maybe the loud, sharp yell was a good idea, plainly separating a command from casual conversation among hunters—and definitely singling out Clyde from several other dogs. It began to appear that this Brittany had a pretty good program and needed no interference from me.

Then came the dead-bird business, generally related to retrieving. Clyde had his own attitude toward this situation. A bunch of Huns flushed wild from somewhere over a rocky rise, where I assume Clyde had tried to pin them. The birds flew down over the hill, where I could watch them, and dropped into heavy grass and weeds only a couple of hundred yards from me. It was the kind of cover Huns seldom go into unless badly spooked. Clyde showed up promptly, calmly surveying the scene, but had no idea where to look for them. I didn't try to direct him but simply walked toward the birds, which had split into two distinct groups.

A pair flushed almost at my feet, heading straight up out of the thick stuff. They shook me so much that I led them too far at close range—then tried to correct my error and missed them dramatically at about twenty yards. As an excuse, I'll plead that I hadn't been Hun hunting for a long time. Clyde accepted the situation calmly, as if he'd expected me to miss. Then he walked softly toward where some of the other birds had landed. They'd evidently moved out of the heaviest grass and I guess Clyde pointed. Anyway, he stopped and faced calmly toward where the birds had gone and looked about for his gun bearer. He could have been waiting for a bus.

I like this next part because I looked pretty good. Two birds flushed ahead of Clyde, about thirty-five yards from me. One swung across the steep face of the hill, and I got it. Clyde ran to where it had fallen and stood there as if to mark the spot. I told him to fetch, but the term seemed unfamiliar to him. He didn't pick up anything. Then the second bird flushed and dived downhill. It was almost forty yards away, but I centered that one too and noted a white streak heading toward where it fell. When Clyde got there he appeared to lose interest and stared off over the valley, where a distant town and a shiny river made for a scenic view.

Not sure the bird was finished, I lost my cool and started yelling for Clyde to hunt dead. Apparently these were strange words to him; he merely maintained his serene observation of the valley. When I got there I was sputtering, but, as I reached for his collar, I noted the dead bird lying between his front feet. Clyde did not exactly point those dead birds; he marked them. Could it be he had adopted that strategy rather than scuffle with other dogs that wanted to retrieve?

Anyway, Clyde changed his program a little later. The next time there was a dead bird he found it in a stubble field, stood and held it gently for a while, and looked around to see if anyone else was interested. When he saw me coming toward him and talking retrieving, he decided he might as well bring the bird to me, which he did.

A large percentage of gun dogs do not retrieve naturally, and we all know that delivering the bird to hand is actually discouraged in some forms of hunting. I have a feeling that Clyde had habitually deferred to another dog in the retrieving business. As long as he stood over dead birds or pointed them, I was inclined to let him do it his way. I'm pretty certain he could be force-broken into classier retrieving, but he's fairly soft. Is it possible that force work might discourage him from hunting dead, especially if other dogs are with him? The persistent dead hunter is a treasure; the attention span of most dogs ranges from seconds to hours.

Some might fault Clyde for his style, but the demand for a "high head" seems a little shaky to me. I'd think the dog's head should be where the scent is, and if it's low to the ground in a high wind, then that's where it should be collected. Although "foot scent" is spoken of only in furtive whispers in some circles, I still think tracking is often essential with running birds of several varieties. In a stubble field, Clyde went some distance with his nose near the ground (horrors!), then suddenly lifted his snout (obviously catching body scent) and proceeded for some distance before he pointed. It was as if the whole thing had become boring. I cheer when a dog "slams" into a point, but I would rather see one sneak than risk busting the birds.

I like style, but I'm on Clyde's side.

BEN O. WILLIAMS is a native of Illinois, but he transplanted his family to Livingston, Montana in the 1950s, following a four-year hitch in the U.S. Navy. He taught in the public school systems of Illinois, Montana, and Washington for twenty-seven years and was the architect of forty homes in the Livingston area. In addition, Ben's bronze, ceramic, and steel sculptures have been exhibited throughout the United States. He has also been a professional photographer for twenty years, specializing in upland birds and gun dogs—notably Brittanys.

Ben is a columnist for *The Pointing Dog Journal,* a contributing editor for *Gray's Sporting Journal* and *Montana Big Sky Journal,* and a freelance writer and photographer for *Alaska, Field & Stream, Montana Outdoors, Pheasants Forever,* and *Shooting Sportsman.* He has written four books: *Wingshooter's Guide to Montana, Wingshooter's Guide to South Dakota, Western Wings,* and *American Wingshooting.*

Ben has bred, trained, and hunted Brittanys for more than forty years. As this is written, he has a kennel full of pointing dogs—twelve Brittanys, two pointers, and one English setter. His Brittany Clyde is the subject of Charley Waterman's story "Me and Clyde" (page 169).

"The Dog No One Wanted" is an original piece not previously published. "Brittanys Hunting in the West" is an excerpt from an article that first appeared in *The Pointing Dog Journal,* September/October 1998. "Clyde" is an expanded version of a story that was first published in *The Pointing Dog Journal,* January/February 2000.

The Dog No One Wanted

by Ben O. Williams

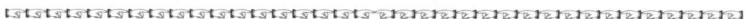

Of all the animals, bird dogs—and more specifically the pointing breeds—are the most interesting to me. No man can learn all the complexities or behavioral characteristics of a particular pointer, and every dog's personality is different. But, with an open mind, deep interest, maturity, companionship, and teamwork, both man and dog can become better hunters. To fully understand an animal that points birds has driven me for the past half century. To me, when a dog locks up on point it's mystical. I am still learning, even after working with more than a hundred dogs of my own.

In my late teens, I set aside my favorite gun, hung up my tattered hunting coat, and said good-bye to my springer spaniel, Mike. The Korean War (they called it a "conflict") interrupted my bird hunting. Instead of being drafted, I joined the United States Navy. At sea, getting a letter sometimes took months. Word finally came, "Mike the dog passed away." But I still have a vivid memory of him and me hunting together. In my mind I can see him flushing a covey of bobwhite quail, me subconsciously bringing the muzzle of the .410 shotgun up, and hearing the loud report. Mike did his job to the best of his ability, but I'm not sure I did mine.

After serving a four-year hitch in the military, I enrolled for the fall semester at Northern Illinois University.

It's August fifteenth, and I'm driving a yellow '51 Chevy convertible, trying to follow an old map with my finger and the gravel road with my eyes. Outsiders consider this former tallgrass prairie monotonous, calling it a land of nothing but fallow fields and standing corn. I like the place. The unhurried, section-line roads—grids I call them—are the way to see the landscape. Ten-foot-high green corn is divided by a narrow strip of gravel. On each side is a wide, grassy barrow pit and brush-lined wire fencing that locks in the corn. Each mile I slow down. The road is only visible straight ahead, but curved wheel ruts indicate an intersection. First I turn right, then—farther on—left, zigzagging from west to north. Beyond every turn young pheasants are chasing insects along the dusty gravel. They are in no hurry to leave as I go by.

At noon I'm waiting for the Texaco station attendant to fill the gas tank of my car. Dekalb, Illinois, is a small, quiet farming community known nationally for its DeKalb hybrid corn. But to me this is a pheasant-hunting paradise. The attendant cleans the dust off the car windows. I pay him $3.25 for the gas and ask about living quarters. He hands me the local newspaper and says, "At this time of year there's all kinds of housing available."

By sundown I'm settling in, thinking about looking for a place to hunt and for a hunting companion. Opening day is less than three months away. Yet without a bird dog it won't be the same. I read that English pointers and

English setters have always been the most popular pointing breeds for the upland hunter. Never having owned a pointer, it seems the English setter would be best for pheasant country.

Next morning, I'm drinking coffee and reading the morning news. A newspaper ad gets my attention: "Two-year-old English setter, to give away. Call after five." The ad excites me, I can hardly wait until five o'clock.

At the specified hour I start dialing. A man answers the phone. I explain my interest in the English setter for bird hunting.

"Sir," he says, "we've had second thoughts about giving the dog away. I've never hunted him, he's our pet, and the family has decided to keep him." The man apologizes, then informs me that west of town, on Highway 30, a man has a kennel full of dogs. When he drove by, some looked like setters.

It's 5:20, and an elderly gentleman answers the door, I introduce myself as a new student who has just moved to town. I tell him that I heard he raised English setters and that I'm interested in buying one.

"Sorry son, I do not raise setters, but I do have pointing dogs."

I'm about to leave when he asks, "Would you care to see them?"

I hesitate, but for some reason I say yes.

"Come with me," I go along just to see what kind of dogs he has. But my thoughts are still on an English setter.

He opens the first kennel gate and calls out. "Mike!" several times.

A beautiful, long-legged, orange-and-white dog runs to

him, puts his front paws on the man's chest, and wags his short tail. Mike is magnificent. "What kind of a dog is he?" I ask.

"He's a Brittany spaniel, a pointing breed from Brittany, in France." Proudly Mr. Oberlin says, "When the war ended, I was one of the first to bring them to the United States. They're great dogs."

Mike, comes to me and jumps up, his hazel-colored eyes sparkling with enthusiasm. He wags his tail, jumps down, and runs toward the house. He's the first Brittany I've ever seen.

"May I see the others?" I ask.

Mr. Oberlin turns to me, knowing that I like dogs, and says, "You look older than most beginning students, were you in the military?"

"Yes sir, spent four years in the navy."

"Being in college, how do you plan on keeping a dog?" he asks.

I answer, "I'm not sure, but I'll find a way."

He smiles and asks if I plan on getting a part-time job.

"I get the GI bill, but I also plan to work some," I said

"How would you like to come and work for me?" he asks. "You can put in whatever hours you want. I'm retired, travel a lot, and need someone to take care of the dogs when I'm gone. You could also work them. A young man has been helping me, but he graduated and left town."

"Sir, I don't know anything about training dogs." I answer.

"Neither did he when he started," Mr. Oberlin states. "With Brittanys you don't have to. All you have to do is take them out and run 'em. The dogs do the rest. I run dogs and hunt just about everyplace in this county, and you can too, if you help me. I'll see to that. Now, about buying a dog. If you work here you won't need a dog; you can hunt one or two of mine. And if you stay, I'll give you a couple of pups when you graduate," Mr. Oberlin says, with a big grin.

Walter Oberlin presented me with the opportunity, the knowledge, and the gift of a lifetime—he showed me how man and dog share the hunting experience. Today I have twelve Brittanys, all an extension of his bloodlines—some old, some young, but every one a good hunter. Certain dogs stand out in my memory. One was from Oberlin Kennels—Michael McGillicuddy, named by my friend Charley Waterman. McGillicuddy did it all.

Daisy and Chantilly I purchased from Jim Leverick's Tip Top Kennels in Pampa, Texas. Jim's Brittanys are big-running, field-trial dogs. McGillicuddy and Daisy become the foundation of my brood lines at Williams' Pride Kennels. Both dogs became natural hunters—just what Walter Oberlin considered to be good breeding stock.

Out of Williams' Pride Michelangelo and Williams' Pride Daisy came Williams' Pride Leo. He was a mostly white, wide-ranging dog and a great bird finder. I bred him to Chantilly. Her first litter—two males and four females—was mostly white. Five of the pups had the typical, orange-colored Brittany ears. The sixth was an all-white male with one orange ear. He was not a handsome pup and was extremely shy.

At that time, I had no plans of establishing a bloodline with this breeding. I sold the first pup at seven weeks, and after another week the litter got pretty well picked over. No one wanted "White Ear." But the little ball of fur would not take his eyes off me. I would place an old white shoe alongside him, and he would wag his little white tail, stretch out, and close both eyes. Side by side, they looked like a pair of tennis shoes. I called him Shoe.

At that time he was nine weeks old. I had no intention of keeping a pup from the litter, but sometimes a youngster chooses you. At night, Shoe slept with the old tennis shoe; during the day he followed my shoes. He helped me dig in the garden and walked behind the riding mower while I cut the lawn. Even at that young age he never took his eyes off me.

One day, although Shoe was running out front, he could not keep up with my five adult Brittanys. But even at four months old, he tried. I kept walking and dropped into a low swale, so Shoe could not see me. Then I stopped to find out if he would follow the other dogs or come and look for me. Shoe did neither; he just howled. I reappeared, and he ran to me, wagging his tail.

I like pups to run at a young age, but I also like them to be aware of my location. A young dog is usually more obedient in the field because it's unfamiliar country, so he depends on his master. In this way a pup learns that checking in is important.

I consider myself a dog breeder, not a professional dog trainer. After working with Walter Oberlin, I moved to Montana. I began to selectively breed Brittanys for hunting the big open prairie. I don't do yard drills with them. All my training is done at the dogs' leisure, in big open spaces, and always on wild game birds. When a pup is four or five months old, I take him along with the self-trained dogs so that the pup learns from them. When a youngster figures out that he can't catch the birds, he watches the other dogs and starts to self-break. I'm very big on natural field training and letting the dog use its innate hunting ability. In other words, I like to let the dog be a dog.

It's nine months later, and Shoe is a year old. He is running with his sire and dam, Leo and Chantilly. He finds three coveys of Hungarian partridge and two bunches of sharp-tailed grouse on his own. After I scatter the coveys, Shoe points and retrieves. He does it all. Shoe occupies a special niche in my heart. Some say a man only deserves

C. SMITH '00

one great dog in a lifetime, and great pointing dogs do not come along often. Shoe may be the best dog I ever had, but his son Winston is just as good.

Today, I'm running eight of Shoe's offspring. All eight are on point at once. As I walk in to flush the birds, I'm thinking fondly about the dog that no one wanted.

Brittanys Hunting in the West

by Ben O. Williams

It was a cool afternoon in January; in the southern sky, mackerel clouds hung over the isolated range of mountains. My partner, Ben Brown, and I had planned to hunt during midday, and our timing couldn't have been better. The weather was changing rapidly and looked more promising by the minute. The temperature was in the low sixties and dropping, with a moist breeze blowing. The wind seemed to follow the meandering arroyo, and it changed the pickup-tire tracks on the sandy road to snake-like ripples.

Once out of the truck, the Brittanys pushed into the wind and disappeared in the tall rabbit brush. In fact, all of them were out of view before Ben and I had our light 20-gauge shotguns uncased. Ben said the area had not been hunted that season, and the bird reports he'd received from the ranch hands were promising.

Most of the cover was a soft amber color, but still unfriendly. The trees' once-green foliage was down and brown, but the rabbit brush still held its muted, pale green colors. We headed in the direction the dogs had gone, following the sandy road toward the singing windmill.

As we were walking through the high cover, listening to the beeper collars, a single Gambel's quail got up out of the brush at my feet. I didn't mount the gun, but instead marked the bird down on the grassy hillside high above us. I could also see more quail dashing ahead of us on the ground. The Brittanys were pointing and running, pointing and running, their beepers changing to the point mode each time they stopped. We were into a large covey of moving Gambel's quail.

There were quail tracks everywhere in the sand, and the dogs were in hot pursuit following them. After several staunch points, our Brittanys finally caught up with the birds, and a large bunch of running Gambel's rushed into the air with a tremendous roar of wings. They flew in the same direction as the single I had flushed.

I marked several birds down and saw others running up the hillside. The dogs also knew the birds' approximate location, and by the time Ben and I walked up the hill, they were locked up tight. Ben moved in on the first point, and a quail got up and peeled off down the hill. At the shot, the bird tumbled and feathers drifted down, following the current of wind that hugged the contour of the rocky hill. Ben admired the bird for a while before he slid it into his vest.

Between the two of us, we collected a bird or two more out of the covey, then decided to look for a new bunch. We found a couple more coveys and took a few more birds.

After circling around to the truck, Ben and I took a moment to appreciate our Gambel's quail. We smoothed their feathers and laid them down in a row, their top-knot feathers casting long shadows on the sand.

Clyde

by Ben O. Williams

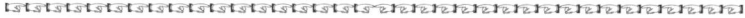

Canine characters don't come along often, but my Brittany Clyde is a character. He is named after Clyde Park, Montana, which was originally Madame Bulldog's stage stop and rest station. With the establishment of the post office, the new town was named Clyde Park—Clyde, after several ranchers in the area raised Clydesdale horses imported from England; Park, because the valley had a park-like appearance.

The name Clyde fits the dog well. He's built like a bulldog and can run like a horse, but he would be just as happy lying around greeting folks getting off a stagecoach.

With three hard hunting seasons under his collar, Clyde points, backs, honors other canine hunting partners, finds downed birds, and retrieves them. When hunting with other dogs, he locates his share of coveys and works singles well. In field-trial terms, I'd call him a steady pointer, but not necessarily a finished performer. He's never been top dog in my kennel—nor second, for that matter—but he does make the "A" team occasionally. Clyde's good, but he will never be a great dog. He could be, but his character gets in the way. Some days he's a dependable hunter; other times he's a clown and screws around when he should be working.

Clyde likes to travel. That is, ever since Charley Waterman's wife, Debie, provided the dog with a traveling companion.

In telephone conversations with Charley, bird dogs and bird hunting are frequently the main topic of discussion. Not having had a dog for a couple of years, Charley had been seriously thinking of getting a trained pointing dog to hunt those little southern bobwhite quail he likes so much. After I suggested he could use Clyde, Charley offered to buy him. I refused, saying nobody was going to buy Clyde, but I explained that he could have the dog on permanent loan. After a lengthy discussion, Charley accepted. Clyde had almost completed his fourth fall bird-hunting season and like Montana snowbirds—folks that also have a home in the south—he left for Florida after the first snowflake fell.

Charley picked up Clyde at the airport. The dog quickly decided that he and Charley had hit it off fairly well and that he should be by his new master's side at all times. Now, Debie had fixed up the backyard for Clyde's arrival—supplying a dog house, shady kennel run, large exercise yard, various squeaky toys, and a bucket full of doggie biscuits. Clyde spent his first day with Charley, but that evening Debie escorted him to his new home in the backyard. Unfortunately, Clyde took a dim view of being alone in his southern canine mansion. Unhappy being out back, he howled his opinion, informing the neighbors that he lived with other dogs and people in Montana and did not like being by himself.

Debie had no intention of letting Clyde take up permanent residence in the house. She figured that snowbirds go south for a reason. The winters are mild there, with warm nights, so Clyde shouldn't have a beef about living in the dog house.

After several neighbors started cutting their lawns with noisy power mowers during unusual hours and when the city police began cruising by the house more than usual, Charley and Debie knew they had to do something about Clyde's barking problem. He clearly needed a companion, but having two dogs was out of the question. After several more nights of coyote cadence, Debie came up with a plan, and that Saturday morning, she left the house early to go yard-sale shopping, hoping to find a cure for Clyde's all-night howling.

Driving around looking for good yard sales not only takes time but also enormous quantities of gasoline, enough to cancel out otherwise good bargains. But Debie was looking for only one item, even though several other good buys caught her attention. With the gas-gauge needle leaning on empty, all but a few newspaper yard-sale ads not crossed out, and most of the city streets covered, Debie finally hit it big time and found a yard sale with a table full of children's stuffed animals. The object she had been looking for stared her in the eyes. It was a large, white, fleece polar bear with a black nose and small black, beady button eyes. Sitting on the edge of the table, its head drooping, the bear seemed to be waiting for a new companion. Debie scooped it up, paid the lady a buck, stopped at the nearest gas station, fueled up, and headed home with the prize.

By this time the sun had set, both Charley and Clyde were hungry, and the bit about being full-time buddies was wearing rather thin with Charley. After a hardy meal,

Clyde—being very tired—accepted the stuffed bear as one of his own canine friends, quit howling, and slept. In fact, from then on, the neighborhood's nights were normal again.

Clyde hunted two bobwhite seasons, but the good quail hunting had plummeted in Charley's area. Clyde found a few birds, but Charley spent most of the time kicking palmetto clumps and finding box turtles. In the end, he felt a dog of Clyde's stature should have more bird-hunting opportunities.

After being gone two and a half years, Clyde returned to Montana. When I let him out of the large shipping crate, he carried his white bear through the crowded airport baggage area and out the revolving door to the parking lot. Clyde jumped in the pickup truck, placed the bear on the seat, and looked at me as if he had never left home. He soon joined the other dogs in the kennel, and because dogs don't forget one another, he was received warmly. Clyde and his kennel mates subsequently made many hunting trips to other states. The white bear sat in a highchair in the utility room, waiting for Clyde's next trip alone.

It wasn't long in coming but started out with my making plans to go fishing. Three taimen fishing camps had recently opened in Mongolia. I knew that nowhere else on Earth was it possible to catch fish over fifty pounds on dry flies. I booked the trip through Sweetwater Travel Company, owned by the Vermillion brothers.

Jeff Vermillion later called me and asked if I would be interested in looking into the bird-hunting possibilities in Mongolia while I was fishing. During the previous season, Jeff had flushed quite a few partridge while walking the high meadow banks along the river in order to spot large, cruising taimen for his anglers. After seeing so many birds, the camp hosts—Jeff, Pat, and Dan Vermilion—became interested in offering upland hunting to their fishing clients.

Jeff's idea was to get a dog or two, a couple of shotguns, and some ammo for the next season. It seemed to me that buying trained hunting dogs and shipping them to Mongolia was a bit premature for the bird-hunting adventure, so I offered to send Clyde.

I had booked my fishing trip for the first week the camp opened—not the ideal time for hunting game birds. Because the climate there was the same as Montana's, I knew the partridge would be immature and the foliage still green and plentiful. But, because this was an exploratory trip, I was more interested in finding partridge for future hunting.

Clyde and the white bear arrived in camp a week ahead of me. My stay would be six days, while Clyde's would last for the duration of the fishing season, whether we found birds or not.

I was looking forward to shooting a gray partridge on its native soil in Mongolia, not far from the border with Russia. This species was introduced into North America at the turn of the century, and I had shot my first one almost fifty years prior to my trip.

Northern Mongolia is an open, arable landscape that encompasses the temperate grassland ecosystems of the steppes and the mountainous country, with its many lakes and rivers teeming with untouched flora and fauna. It makes me think of what Montana must have been like a hundred and fifty years ago.

The rivers, strings of sapphire jewels, twist though lush valley floors thick with green summer grass and blankets of colorful wildflowers. The mountains that corral the rivers have mixed stands of aspen and larch. As in Montana, fall comes early, with long days of sunshine and brisk, cool nights. Where the rivers bend, forming oxbows or islands, the land is flat, with thick vegetation and strings of willows. This is where the Mongolian subspecies of the gray partridge, the Darwinian partridge, lives.

I got out of the helicopter, expecting to see Clyde jumping with joy at my presence, but there was no dog in sight. Jeff escorted me to my home away from home, a large tentlike structure called a *ger*. A young Mongolian walked alongside carrying my grip. When I entered the camp, Clyde recognized me but did not move. He stood by the front door of the fishing guide's ger and wagged his tail. This puzzled me—why was he so standoffish? The young Mongolian put my grip in the ger, and it wasn't until he left that Clyde—carrying the white bear—greeted me. He jumped on the extra bed—again, with the bear—and watched me unpack.

Later Jeff explained that for some unknown reason, Clyde had taken a disliking to the Mongolian employees in camp. He would not look at them nor recognize their presence. Clyde has always liked the ladies, but he would not even associate with the lovely Mongolian interpreter or the cook, of all people. Other than that, however, Clyde seemed to love having free run of the camp and mixing with the guides and the guests.

Our experimental bird-hunting effort did have its difficulties. No hunting gear had arrived, and Jeff was a little reluctant to show me the camp shotgun he had gotten from his Mongolian partner. Firearms—let alone ammunition—are difficult to come by in Mongolia, but I finally did get my hands on the shotgun. Tongue in cheek, I called it, "the Russian Purdey." The single-shot, full-choke, 16-gauge opened reluctantly. But other than being a bit corroded, it did fire. Similar to a lever action, a release in back of the trigger guard opened the breech. The $2\frac{3}{4}$-inch paper Russian shotshells were available in my choice of BBs (fifty-four pellets) and #1s (seventy-two pellets)—hardly the ideal shot size for small upland game birds.

With no maintained roads and a hundred miles of river, a jet boat is the best transportation for finding birds. Every open meadow along the water's course potentially held partridge. Clyde took a dim view of his first ride afloat, but after making the connection—boat equals hunting—he would carry the white polar bear down to the river each morning, jump aboard, and patiently wait for me to arrive. Clyde figured that the boat he chose was the one I would use.

As the flat-bottomed boat skipped across the riffles, a spray of fine mist would lift above the bow on every other bounce. Clyde kept his head down, on the bear, under a tarp. Seated, I took the brunt of it. As we passed meadows I looked for willow tops above the high banks. At every likely spot Jeff would slow or stop so that we could check out the partridge cover. Each time he throttled back, Clyde would raise his head and look at me, then turn to shore, as if he knew something that we didn't.

At one likely looking spot, Jeff eased the boat into shore. The high, rocky bank obscured the meadow above, but last year he had found partridge here. When I scurried up the incline, the meadow didn't look much different than the other ones we had passed, except there were more lines of willows, eight to ten feet high, following the low swales like fingers reaching into the lush, green field. The meadow's backdrop—a low, dry, rocky bench that followed the contour of the mountain—was covered with short grass and mixed forbs. In some places the bench was narrow, while in others it was wide, following aspen draws into steep larch slopes.

Jeff carried the "Russian Purdey." He put a handful of shells in the inexpensive hunting vest I had brought for the trip. I also had a beeper collar, which I activated and put on Clyde.

The dog headed for the willows, the beeper sounding every ten seconds. Jeff and I were almost to the first string of willows when the dog turned suddenly, and the beeper changed to the pointing mode. Now, Clyde is not the most classic pointer in my kennel. As Charley Waterman put it, "When Clyde points, he looks as if he's waiting for a bus." But because this was his first point in Mongolia, we hoofed it toward him. The covey flushed under Jeff's feet, too close for #1 shot. We watched the birds fly along the willows and lost them as they hooked through a clearing. As Jeff and I walked toward the opening, two partridge flew over our heads, toward the rest of the covey, with Clyde in hot pursuit. He had apparently found two more birds after the main covey flushed. This pair flew in a straight line, high over the willows, and appeared to settle down not far beyond.

"They act just like Montana Huns," I said. "The late risers follow a straight course to catch up to the rest of the bunch. I believe those two birds just told us where the rest of the covey landed."

Clyde ran through the clearing in the thick willows. Fifty yards beyond the trees, he slowed in a brushy patch, then stopped. He had 'em. The covey flushed, flying over our heads, scattering like autumn leaves in a windstorm. Turning completely around, Jeff shot and dropped a bird just short of the willows. Clyde crashed though the thicket, running over the downed bird, and I called him back to hunt dead. He found the partridge, scooped it up, looked at me, then eyed the boat. It seems his thoughts were elsewhere—like on lunch. I admired the young Darwinian partridge before Jeff slipped it into his vest. Walking the quarter mile back to the boat, Clyde found two large coveys, and in return we shared our lunch with him.

My first native partridge came in the afternoon, when the Brittany pointed eight more coveys before we called it quits. Jeff and I went fishing; Clyde slept.

Six weeks later, Jeff called and said that he, Clyde, and the stuffed polar bear had arrived safely in Billings, Montana. The trip back to the United States for Clyde and the bear was a piece of cake. Jeff said that the hunting had been outstanding and that Clyde had performed well in the field. He also told me that there had been an incident involving the dog and several Mongolians.

At the camps, Thursday is turnover day. A Miat—a Mongolian airline helicopter—brings six new fishing guests and returns the previous fishing party to Ulaabaatar. For each new group, a special traditional Mongolian meal called *hairhog* is prepared. The food is cooked outdoors in a metal drum. A lamb is slaughtered, cut into large pieces, and placed carefully in the container, separated by round, very hot river rocks. Then the metal container is slipped into the larger metal drum, which sits in a bed of hot coals. A top is added to the drum, and the meat is slow-cooked all day.

Clyde always watched this process with great interest. The Mongolians first cut up the lamb and placed the large pieces on the ground. Laying out the hot rocks and preparing the container takes time, and little attention is paid to the meat. I'm sure Clyde took this into account.

By the third week he had the routine figured out. The next time the three Mongolians' backs were turned as they laid out the hot rocks, Clyde slipped up very quietly and stole the most prized piece of meat, a large leg of lamb. He then made a beeline for the woods with the three Mongolians in hot pursuit. Clyde vanished among the trees.

Two hours later the Brittany walked into camp, his stomach bulging, and went to sleep in his assigned ger. Most of the guides moved out that night. Jeff said that after Clyde's wonderful meal of leg of lamb and the absence of a reprimand, the dog finally took a liking to the Mongolians, especially the cook. But I suspect they bribed him with bits of tender lamb.

Clyde and his kennel mate, Patagonia, are going to the fishing camp in Mongolia next fall. With Pat along, I think maybe the white polar bear will stay home.

RALPH HAMMOND, along with his brother, Robert, wrote a book entitled *Training and Hunting the Brittany Spaniel*. It was published in 1971 by A.S. Barnes Company, which is no longer in business, and included the following poem, "The Ballad of Fabulous Floyd."

We made an extensive telephone search in an effort to locate either Ralph or Robert Hammond, or relatives who might possibly live in the Tulsa, Oklahoma, and Wichita, Kansas, areas. We were not successful but thought Ralph's piece was a fitting way to end our celebration of the Brittany. We hope he would think so, too.

The Ballad of Fabulous Floyd

by Ralph Hammond

Now I've always been a pointer man and love that fiery
    breed
But I'm hunting now the Brittany to satisfy a need
For the hunting lands of nowadays no longer stretch so far
It's a forty here and eighty there and long trips in the car

I often met with the pointer men who used to hunt with
    me
Whose friendly arguments took the place of hunting
    rhapsody
In time a meeting came about to decide which breed was
    best
The Brittany or the pointer and for that we had to test

By luck a holiday came about between two hunting days
Giving us the needed time to pursue our hunting craze
The birds we'd shoot from each dog's point was the plan
    agreed to weigh
The merits of our favorite breed and all we'd have to say

The place we chose to stage our hunt was extremely rough
and vast
A hilly, rocky, valleyed ranchland, a relic of the past
The course we'd picked was broad and long, suiting best
wide range and speed
They but little cared but soon would know the toughness
of my breed

The first day's hunt brought even scores from covey rise
and singles
'Twas very tough on man and dog, the yield was thirty
bingles
What makes so easy these quail to flush and run ahead
like fiends
The birds that fly from a point are killed, the rest pass on
their genes

The pointer men amazed to find the Brittany hangin' tough
Were quick to state that tomorrow's hunt would surely be
too rough
My two friends' dogs were veterans both, two pointers
hard to beat
Trained, experienced, and conditioned to run an all-day heat

The hunt they ran was a beauty, with the pointer work
superb
The Brittany pushed on, driving hard, o'er rock and brush
and herb
They whipped the deep wide valley dry, seeking out the
quarry's lair

The sound of our guns like thunder rolled in the crisp
    winter's air

Back and forth across the frozen creek, vibrant in the bright
    sun
Pressed on our driving charges, fired up by the sound of the
    gun
The Brittany handled singles best and coveys overrun
T'was plain for all to see—he was a hunting son of a gun

The pointers slowed the second day the Brittany held his
    pace
As time went by he gained the lead and began to win the
    race
The third day of the grueling hunt ground the pointers to a
    walk
At noon they faltered, limping, but the Brittany did not
    balk

This dog is not run of the mill, tho' he's Britt'ny thru and
    thru
His breeding traits have been enhanced, he excels in all
    they do
I've seen him hunt with a tender foot on three legs with-
    out rest
Tough bottomed, alert to scent, with hunting desire at its
    best

I've hunted him with good hunting dogs the best that can
    be found

An' there ain't a dog a livin' that can hunt him in the
    ground
He's a legend to all who've seen him, his guts have won
    him fame
He's a wondrous, zestful gun dog—Fabulous Floyd is his
    name